Discovering
The Pentland Hills

Other titles in this series

Discovering
The Pentland
Hills

JIM CRUMLEY

JOHN DONALD PUBLISHERS LTD
EDINBURGH

For George Garson
Friend of these hills.

ISBN 0 85976 331 5

British Library Cataloguing in Publication Data
Crumley, Jim 1947-
   Discovering the Pentland hills.
   1. Lothian (Scotland)
   2. Title
914.135

Phototypeset by Newtext Composition Ltd, Glasgow.
Printed & bound in Great Britain by Scotprint Ltd, Musselburgh.

Contents

Acknowledgements

The author would like to acknowledge all those writers who have dipped their pens in the Pentland Wine over the centuries, but notably Will Grant and George M. Reith, whose benevolent ghosts have kept me company over many a glad Pentlands mile.

Thanks to Scotsman Publications for the use of several photographs.

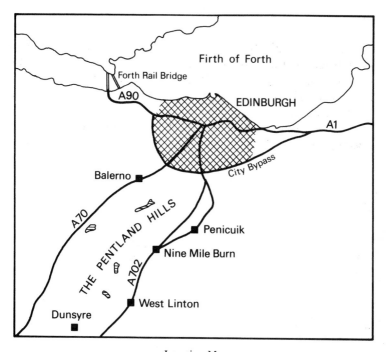

Location Map

The Gardener of Verses

Louis your ghost
is everywhere among
the small crushed mountains
of the Pentlands.

How else explain
plashing footfalls
in the syke
where no foot falls?

Or wind's ambush
in Ravens Cleuch's immortal
stillness – (a laughing
spirit's breath)?

Who else hovers
copper-kestrel-bright
overhead? Or leapfrogs
eyebright underfoot?

Or shifts all
quick-silvering things
the will-o'-the-whisperers
that stitch the seamless

and seemly garments
of the Pentland Hills
a child puts on to go
gardening for verses?

Jim Crumley
Cauldstane Slap, 1990.

CHAPTER 1

The Pentland Wine

And for the simple wayfarer with a hunger in his heart which only the hills can satisfy, there is the wide heaven above and the open road before him that leads to his Arcadia, where amidst the glorious hills he enjoys the pleasure he counts the best; for he knows the fragrant perfume the spring wind carries, he enjoys the smile of wayside flowers, and the cheery song and echoing cry of birds, and through the senses his heart is touched. He it is who at the day's end will say that his life is good, that he is satisfied, for that he has found a new song wherewith to sing the praises of a new land in the Pentland Hills.

There has been no new book of any substance about the Pentland Hills for more than sixty years. The above extract is from Will Grant's *The Call of the Pentlands* which appeared in 1927, and although he published a collection of newspaper and magazine articles a few years later as *Pentland Days and Country Ways*, it was an altogether slighter and more haphazard book, and *The Call of the Pentlands* stands as the last milestone in the literature of these hills.

It is a surprising gap considering the Pentland's literary pedigree. What other range of hills which fails to top 2000 feet has been acclaimed by such as Robert Louis Stevenson (who carried memories and images of the Pentlands across the world with him like a talisman, and to his grave), Allan Ramsay, Robert Burns, Lord Cockburn, John Ruskin, and the obligatory Scott? There are lesser names too like George M. Reith, a cheerful swiper at convention and authority whose 1910 publication, *The Breezy Pentlands*, is a wry and entrancing period piece, and Robert Cochrane's *Pentland Walks with their Literary and Historical Associations* of 1930.

Stevenson is the irresistible prince among all these, and some of his later letters to friends in Edinburgh vividly and almost painfully evoke the Pentlands of his youth. But it is

Will Grant who seems to have poured his life into the Pentlands. He didn't just love the hills and wax lyrical about them, he *knew* them in all their seasons, and he cared about them; although he occasionally regurgitated chunks of Reith without attributing them, his book had a style and a flair and a feeling for the wildness of the Pentland Hills. He was nowhere in Stevenson's class as a writer, but *The Call of the Pentlands* is no meagre memorial, either to Grant or to the Pentlands of his day. It is still reasonably available in good secondhand bookshops: I recommend it highly. Yet it is inevitably of its time, and Grant would find the Pentlands of today so changed that his confusion would be equalled only by his outrage, for little that has changed has changed for the better.

The encroachment of the city, the growth of commuter traffic, the old villages swollen by bad bungalows, the bureaucracy of a regional park and two country parks, bulldozed roads, bad forestry, the invasions of the Army, the trampling erosion of hordes of technicolour walkers, the hill shepherds who drive to work on motor bikes and other moor-gouging vehicles, the demise of the railway, the Hillend ski slope, mountain bikes, a countryside ranger service … All these, and in no particular order of significance, have changed the character of the hills, and whether by accident or design, have diluted their wildness.

Yet much is as it was. Stevenson's 'spiry, habitable city' still tilts engagingly away from the hills' skirts to the sea, a gaggle of good inns still sit inviting and snug under the hills, ragged choirs of moorland birds still stop your heart in its tracks anywhere from Allermuir to Dunsyre Hill, Covenanting ghosts still stravaig the Cauldstane Slap, the sudden underfoot magic of cloudberry still banishes the sodden August greyness of the summit of West Cairn Hill. The Pentlands still throw panoramas over more counties and more shapes and sizes of landscapes than any other hills of such modest size in the land.

And in the embrace of their small mountain shapes and wide moors and cleuchs and sykes and crags and crannies they still swill their history and their natural history into a unique distillation, a heady brew which the Borders poet Will H. Ogilvie christened 'The Pentland Wine':

Up here with the clean winds blowing
I look for you, City of mine,
I fill me a goblet o'erflowing
And pledge you in Pentland wine!
With a full heart filled by your story,
While the hills stand round like kings,
I drink to your lasting glory
In the wine that the hill-wind brings!

Still there are so many pressures on today's Pentland Hills and their fragile wildness, and there are those who will argue that a new book now will only fuel pressures and exacerbate the demise of wildness. Yet our hills have always had a literary tradition, and at its traditional best it has stood us and our landscape in good stead. All of us who walk in Scotland's wild places today are shaped in some way by that tradition. In the Pentlands, Grant is its champion. Further afield, I owe a lot to such as Seton Gordon, W. H. Murray, Brenda Macrow, Tom Weir, Syd Scroggie, Alastair Borthwick, Nan Shepherd, Mike Tomkies ... these and others who wrote books which turned my head and shaped my attitude towards the wilds.

If there is one thing which is conspicuously wrong in the Pentland Hills in the 1990s, it is our attitude towards them, and in writing this book – not a guidebook in any sense but a thoughtful sampling of the Pentland wine – I hope I can suggest a better attitude, and one which stands in the mainstream of our singularly Scottish tradition of going to the hills.

George Reith justified his 1910 book thus: 'After a fruitless search for books of the kind, I came to practical agreement with the philosopher who said that if you cannot find a book on the subject that interests you, you should sit down and write one yourself.' So I did, and here it is. May it serve the cause of the wildness of the Pentland Hills, and the fine hillgoing tradition into which I was mercifully born.

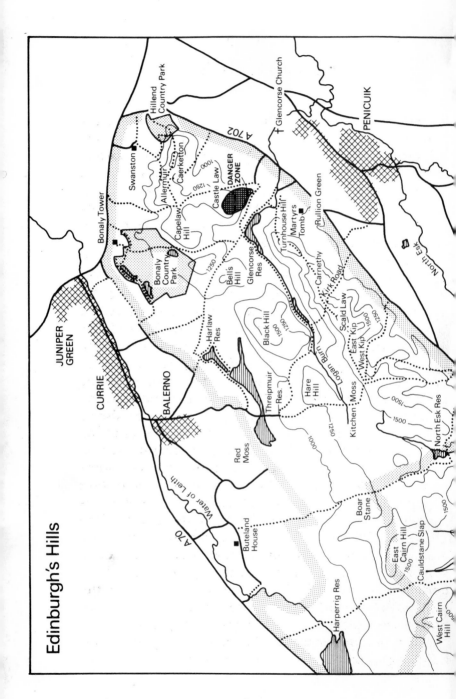

Edinburgh's Hills

JUNIPER GREEN

CURRIE

BALERNO

Water of Leith

A70

Buteland House

Harperrig Res

Red Moss

Threipmuir Res.

Harlaw Res

Bonaly Country Park

Bells Hill

Bonaly Tower

Swanston

Hillend Country Park

Allermuir

Caerketton

Capelaw Hill

Castle Law

DANGER ZONE

1000

1250

1250

A702

Glencorse Church

PENICUIK

Glencorse Res

Turnhouse Hill

Martyrs Tomb

Rullion Green

Carnethy

Kirk Road

Scald Law

East Kip

West Kip

1500

1250

Black Hill

1050

1600

Hare Hill

Logan Burn

Kitchen Moss

Boar Stane

1000

1250

1500

1500

North Esk Res

East Cairn Hill

1500

Cauldstane Slap

West Cairn Hill

1500

North Esk

4

CHAPTER 2

Edinburgh's Hills

Sometimes the first week in December can feel like a month. Such a week, a relentless dirge of iced westerlies, bruise-black skies and squalid squalls of everything wet and wintry, has Edinburgh by the throat. I seek out a refuge, a bar-room seat by an acre of wall-to-wall, floor-to-ceiling glass, a window on the storm. The city reels off into the murk like an old drunk. Sometimes even a city as lenient on the eye as Edinburgh can get you down.

Then the city works its recurring miracle.

It starts as abruptly as the sleety hiss stops. The wind has finally heel-and-toed round to the north, and like the audacious grin of a five-year-old gate-crashing a po-faced Covenanters' conspiracy, brashly intrudes on the staid grey legions of the week's skies. The sodden misery of that week backs off, begins to peel back and up, and a shaft of something like that sun you had forgotten could ever shine ploughs a furrow of light through fields of daylight darkness.

Minute by minute, streets emerge glitter-roofed, then a golf course, a factory, the railway, more roofs, until the wind's southerly march has laid bare the bright-as-a-new-pin city. Then with the last gesture of the miracle-weaver's wand, the soft-and-sharp white sculptures of winter hills emerge, the new snow burnish of Allermuir. How often has a city-bruised soul been healed by the sudden balm of the Pentland Hills? How often over how many years, centuries even, has a pair of eyes lifted from street or garret or suburban plot to meet the startling gaze of the hills' northmost prow, and all that it stands for which is the antithesis of the workaday city – wide horizons, bowls of sky, whaup-weep, plover-sigh, and the silent, bog-myrtled air?

It is a unique service the Pentland Hills perform for Edinburgh, a unique distinction they confer on the city, not

5

'It is a unique service the Pentlands perform for Edinburgh.' The bulk of Allermuir dominates the southern edge of the city. The viewpoint is the Post House Hotel, Corstorphine.

Caerketton with Allermuir behind. The two hill shapes have been an irresistible lure to generations of Edinburgh hill-trampers.

just the lifeline they throw to the city's caged hillwalkers but the airy graces they confer on Edinburgh's landscape setting. Many Edinburgh people, and many visitors, who never set foot in the Pentlands' are grateful for their presence. They say, far more authoritatively than any Green Belt signs or any other ambiguous designation which urban bureaucracy can devise: 'The city stops here.' They serve, too, to remind anyone with half an eye for the sensibilities of nature, that no matter how the affairs of the city might oppress, there are sounder, simpler sets of values within reach. There is no more potent symbol of those values than a winter sunrise blackening the profile of Caerketton and Allermuir.

How often I have invoked that symbol when a snatched glance from, say, a traffic jam in Corstorphine has turned my head. It helps, of course, to know that those twins of the Pentlands' northmost thrust can utterly conceal an unbroken chain of kindred hills which peels off south-westwards for twenty-five miles; to know that if you can thrust yourself in your mind from your traffic jam to the summits of Caerketton or Allermuir, the city which now ensnares and antagonises you is suddenly relegated to a thrumming mumble at your feet. Perhaps your traffic jam is a midsummer ordeal by furnace, and you invoke instead that summer wind which makes a boisterous play of the shores of Harper Rig reservoir and scurries on up the Cauldstane Slap, jigging and whistling through the exquisite drystane dykes on the highest slopes of the Cairn Hills. Perhaps a boil of sleet torments your windscreen and your flight of fancy peels back the dazzling and sculpted aftermath of blizzard on the Wolf Craigs. Then the traffic jam unfankles itself and the daftness is done, but that same old seed is germinating in your mind and what Will Grant knew as *The Call of the Pentlands* is in your ear and tugging your sleeve, irresistible as always.

It is an old lure, this relationship between Edinburgh and the Pentlands. Hunting kings like David I and Robert the

Colinton Kirkyard, and the iron mort safe which was placed over a new grave in the days of Burke and Hare to thwart the graverobbers.

Bruce could always find time amid the affairs of State to take horse and hound into the hills, and doubtless the inspiration was the same – the glimpse of the same old mountain profile from a window of the Castle which snapped royal resolve with the seductive scent of the same old temptations.

Doubtless it was the same old mountain profile which prodded Burns and Nasmyth into their celebrated expedition to the Pentlands starting from a High Street tavern at three in the morning.

Grant wrote: 'It is not always easy for city folk to get away to the breezy heights and the sunny moorlands and the sweet-smelling countryside. But how we like to read about it all, how we like to lose ourselves in thought among the hills and moors, and smell the odour that the hill wind brings ...' That is the particular gift of the Pentlands to Edinburgh, their capacity to induce city folk with no more than a glance to lose themselves in thought among the hills. For I know no-one who knows the Pentlands who doesn't also know them well. They command an affection quite unlike any other range of low hills, certainly in Scotland, partly because of their neighbourliness to the city, partly because of their handsome mountain shapes, and partly because they are simply the Pentland Hills, swathed in their own unfingerable mystique. Edinburgh's hill gangrels are spoiled for choice. The Lammermuirs are lonelier, and arguably lovelier. The Moorfoots are higher and mightier. The Ochils, a brief drive across the Forth away, are infinitely more Highland. But none of these are as confiding as the Pentlands, nor are they so celebrated, nor are they so loved.

The Pentlands' scope and scale invite intimate exploration, and their nagging presence in the corner of Edinburgh's eye ensures that the invitation is rarely declined. Edinburgh folk who go to the Pentlands go often, working the same fragments of landscape again and again. It is a recurring theme in all the Pentlands' literature, and it is as true now as it always was. Reith invoked George Eliot: 'To me, [The Pentlands] have acquired what George Eliot calls

Bonaly Tower, built by Lord Cockburn, where he lived in great contentment for the last forty-three years of his life.

'the sweet monotony when everything is known, and loved because it is known ....' Grant invoked Gilbert White: 'White of Selborne in one of his letters says, "Though I have travelled the Sussex Downs upwards of thirty years, yet I still investigate that chain of majestic hills with fresh admiration year by year, and I think I see new beauties each time I traverse it." So, many a walker has found a like bountiful field of wonder and delight in our hills of home, from which new beauty and inspiration seems to spring eternally.' Lord Cockburn invoked himself: 'Warburton says there was not a bush in his garden on which he had not hung a speculation. There is not a recess in the valleys of the Pentlands, nor an eminence on their summits, that is not familiar to my solitude.' Reith, ever the sceptic, commented that ' It is one of my pardonable ambitions to know the Pentlands as well as Lord Cockburn did – or thought he did – though I own not a yard of them, and can erect no bower of bliss on their heathery slopes.' (Cockburn owned twenty acres of them and set up his 'bower' at Bonaly Tower, where he lived for the last forty-three years of his life. It is reasonable to assume

11

that he got to know the Pentlands at least as well as he thought he did).

Stevenson began rather than ended his life on the Pentlands, a now almost legendary relationship with Swanston, a childhood idyll which sustained him throughout his imperfect youth and adulthood. G.K. Chesterton wrote: 'I do not think that time of transition from the Child's Garden of Verses to the Man's Garden of Vows went right with Stevenson.' To that sentiment, Grant added: 'I think it would have gone much worse if there had been no Swanston and no Pentland Hills.'

While that unshakeable truth applies more to Stevenson than most of us, thousands of people of every Edinburgh generation before and since will identify with the sentiment. The Pentlands on the City's threshold have enriched many a city spirit, lightened many a city darkness, eased many a city burden. For all of us, it would have gone much worse if there had been no Pentland Hills.

It is no meagre debt, then, which Edinburgh owes the Pentland Hills. So why do we repay them with insults and injuries, both by the advance of the city onto the very slopes of the hills themselves, and by a barrage of new and self-indulgent threats which see in the hills only a convenience to be exploited, poisoning the Pentland Wine with an almost malicious bitterness?

It is not a new phenomenon, but the pace at which it has accelerated and devastated aspects of the Pentlands is new and alarming. But first, let's go back to Stevenson. He raged against the City's territorial ambitions in his *Picturesque Old Edinburgh* of 1878: 'From Boroughmuirhead ... the road ... passes a toll-bar and issues at once into the open country. Even as I write these words, they are being antiquated in the progress of events, and the chisels are tinkling on a new row of houses. The builders have at length ventured beyond the toll which held them in respect for so long, and proceed to career in these fresh pastures like a herd of colts turned loose. As Lord Beaconsfield proposed to hang an architect

The charm of Swanston is still largely intact. In a house near the old thatched village, the young Robert Louis Stevenson forged happy memories which would colour his whole life.

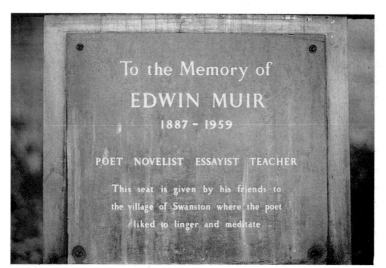

A plaque on a bench at the top of Swanston village commemorates writer Edwin Muir's great fondness for the place as somewhere to sit and think.

by way of stimulation, a man, looking on these doomed meads, imagines a similar example to deter the builders; for it seems as if it must come to an open fight at last to preserve a corner of green country unbedevilled.'

Little could he know just how many more meads were doomed, that within a century of his death you would have to go deep into the Pentlands themselves to find green corners of country unbedevilled. For at the same time, he could still describe Fairmilehead as 'a spot of roof and a smoking chimney, where two roads no thicker than packthread interact beside a hanging wood'.

The city has since submerged Fairmilehead, and cordoned itself off from the upper slopes of the Pentlands with its new bypass and a vile double row of pylons. The cables they carry may be a necessity; the fact that they run their parallel lacerations across the brow of the hills is not. Stevenson said of the view from Caerketton: 'So you sit, like Jupiter upon Olympus, and look down from afar upon men's life.' Not from afar, not any more. The city is right under your feet, even from high on Caerketton; the country lane which once dawdled up to Swanston is now a concrete flyover, a product of the bypass, and of course it must duck under the pylons just before the calming screen of trees parts and maroons you briefly in Swanston.

Swanston? The thatched showpiece is intact enough, although it will never look right with cars parked in its midst, and it's no more village than any other isolated cluster of bonnie houses with no pub, no shop, no kirk, no bus stop, no community focus; the bypass rumbles below and the pylons hum ominously, or so it seems to me, but Caerketton and its pale screes is still the over-lord of the place.

And Stevenson? Well, his star was never brighter. The pilgrims still trauchle up to Swanston Cottage wrapped in its summer green, in search of his lost and fabled childhood,

An intriguing group of old and disused buildings at Hillend. There are many old buildings around the hills which show the skill and sense of place of a forgotten architectural tradition.

or their own. Stevenson wrote it unerringly in his lyric for
the Skye Boat Song:

> Give me again all that was there
> Give me the sun that shone
> Give me the eyes, give me the soul
> Give me the lad that's gone.

Give me the hills that are gone too. I don't mind the
Hillend ski slope, but does it have to be so vulgar and so
untidy? Do the buildings have to be that mock-Swiss timber
cliché of every ski-development the world over when on this
of all hillsides they should be stone and slate? And Scottish?
It is expensive, of course, to build in stone and slate, and it
is expensive to underground pylons. It can be done, though,
and if there was a respect for the landscape, and for that
debt which we all owe the Pentlands, it would be done.
There isn't of course, at least not enough, and not where it
counts, so instead we have repaid the Pentlands with two
country parks and a regional park. These are insidious
interventions of bureaucracy into the management of the
hills, where policies are fashioned by political careerists
remote from the hills. The country parks at Bonaly and
Hillend serve little obvious function other than as focal
points designed to soak up as much punishment as they
inflict on the fabric of the hills. Their creators remain
seemingly blithely oblivious to the fact that crowds go there
because the parks' existence invites them there. Their
potential damage is limited only by the fact that they are
small.

But the land within the parks, and between them, is most
notable for the manner in which it has been utterly tamed.
It is the dullest portion of all the Pentlands. Worse, these
northern slopes of the Pentlands have been made dull,
soiled by policy, shorn of colour by sheep, disfigured by
their own invasion, by the noise of the bypass and the ski
slope, spattered with bureaucracy's handwriting on notices
which warn of 'erosion control'. Reith noted in the first

Hillend ski slope has brought a new bustle to the slopes of the northern Pentlands.

years of the century that ' of late years the golfer has invaded some of the outlying spurs with his quaint pick and shovel'. His paintbrush too, for Lothianburn Golf Club's response to the park's crowds is to patrol its own territorial boundary with 'Trespassers Will be Prosecuted' notices. They won't, of course, but the intimidatory tone is another note of uneasiness on the northern slopes. The hills are no wilder here than Arthur's Seat. In fact Arthur's Seat is arguably wilder because it is not grazed, and by nature's consent, trespasses mutually with the reserves of Duddingston Loch and Bawsinch. The saving grace of the northern slopes of the Pentlands is the view of Edinburgh, which makes them unenviably unique, unenviably because nowhere else in these hills does the view away from them outrank the intrinsic appeal of the hills themselves.

The Pentland Hills Regional Park, however, is an altogether more sinister invention with a far greater potential to wreck the character of the hills. It takes in all the hills from the bypass to the Cauldstane Slap; it is unloved and

A close-up of Hillend ski slope. Courtesy *Scotsman* Publications.

Stevenson's 'spiry, habitable city', with Arthur's Seat prominent, from Caerketton, but now the new bypass severs hills and city like a moat, and new housing champs at the bit, eager to cross it.

unwanted by farmers, landowners, shepherds, local residents, hill wanderers, the great mass of Edinburgh people, in fact by every strand of relevant opinion other than a handful of local authority officials who are paid extravagantly to manage them, and the Countryside Commission for Scotland whose brainchild it was. It is inappropriate, committee-minded, ineffective, expensive, wasteful and utterly useless. Mercifully it plays no part in the Pentlands beyond the Cauldstane Slap, where neither Borders Regional Council nor Strathclyde Regional Council showed any appetite for such an unwieldy and unpopular bureaucratic monster. So the yellow waymarkers, the trite nonsenses about sticking to the path, the patrolling ranger service and the excruciating bureaucratspeak of the park professionals ('leisure resource', 'countryside-users', 'linear walkway') are all missing from the hills beyond the Slap.

They are wilder hills in any case (an inevitable consequence of their distance from the city) and their wildlife is richer. But the northern Pentlands have the charismatic hills, the mountain shapes and the benevolent light of the sea, and for all its thoughtless hamfistedness in the hills, the bittersweet prospect of the handsomest of all Scottish cities, low-slung Edinburgh on its tilting pedestal.

So at Stevenson's bidding, you take your Jupiter-ness up onto the Olympus of Caerketton (and my preference is one of that heady little array of buttresses immediately above the screes where the sheep rarely venture and the ground thickens with heather and blaeberries and the first real hill scents). I find myself pushing back the city's frontiers in my mind, century by century, until it is a gray crouch on its rock, walled against the world, and the Pentlands begin and end with Arthur's Seat. It is a wooded land, a hunter's kingdom, and it rises and falls over the Braid Hills too, for they are still part of the Pentlands in spirit, as they once were as a matter of physical fact. Small huddles of houses gather only at a crossroads, around a coaching inn, or by some sheltered haven on the Lothian shore. The Pentlands about my feet and over my shoulder are wooded too, and a higher upthrust of wilderness in an undulating plain of wilderness.

The city has changed all that. My meandering mind's eye unfurls it again, century by century, a spreading gray stain in every direction at once, chisel-tinkling past Stevenson's Boroughmuirhead, engulfing the Braids, obliterating every discernible village in sight, spread-eagling along the shore. Now the Edinburgh bypass severs hills and city like a moat, and new houses charge to the city's new frontier, champing at the bit to cross it. How long will the bypass hold Edinburgh in check on the foothills of the Pentlands? Perhaps, at last, Edinburgh has built for itself a psychological barrier which planners (certainly not developers) will feel uncomfortable about crossing, in which case, it will be the first time in its considerable history that Edinburgh has limited itself. It still grows to the east and west, and as they'll tell you down Newhaven way, there has been an uncomfortable enthusiasm in recent years to push north deeper into the Firth of Forth.

A ragged stand of Scots pines by the old Water Board hut at Glencorse. Like most of the Pentlands woods, it's a sparse and unhealthy remnant.

The Castle folds down into the mass of the city from high on Caerketton, and there is neither a sense of the Old Town on its rock nor of the peaks and troughs of what is after all a hilly city. Its contours are ironed flat by the psychological impositions on the view of a series of emphatic horizontals. Edinburgh itself is a long east-west city, but it is the impact of the swathe of the firth and the low and dark Fife coast beyond which play those tricks on your eyes that flatten Edinburgh. The river is an immense influence, not just on the lie of the land, but on the light too, and on the insinuation of the sea into the mind and eye of the hillman.

It is, as every explorer of the West Highlands knows, an irresistible mix, and even if there is all Lothian between foothills and shore, there is enough in the Forth's scattering of islands – Inchkeith, the Bass Rock, the Isle of May – to turn any head seawards.

At the centre of it all, though, is the small mountain which, to its eternal credit, the city has cherished at its heart, and for all that it has been a mite careless with the hills across the threshold, Arthur's Seat is Edinburgh's irresistible centrepiece. It never seems to be lit quite the same as the rest of the city. Here is a moment, for example, with the city sombre as a General Assembly in full session, when a vivid yellow lance of light pierces the clouds and turns Salisbury Crags into a tropical fantasy. Arthur's Seat itself, however, is afflicted by the city's stale grayness, until a second yellow lance strikes the same preposterous colour in the mane of its crouched lion profile. Over the next ten minutes the lances rain down on the hill as the sky's resolve weakens, until they are as thick as the twigs of a forester's besom, and all Arthur's Seat is patched with the colour of canaries. There is a moment when a pale wash of the same outrageous shade gilds a square mile of rooftops, but such an un-Edinburgh colour was never likely to catch on, and it snuffs itself almost at once. The impression, though, was that the dozing city dusk had briefly opened an eye, that it had caught and held a glimmer of the show on Arthur's

Seat, that the city, having observed and admired its show-piece at its most skittish, closed the approving eye and dozed off again.

When the sky mustered its resources and switched off the lights again, the city was the same calm gray, but Arthur's Seat of the tropical yellow fire was now a breathless black, a formidable shape of beast which seemed to pant.

Edinburgh's ragged-edged excursions into the fields about its fringes create the illusion that the countryside is reaching deep into the stone heart of the place, rather than the other way round. From such an eyrie as Caerketton's buttresses you appreciate how much the subtle landscape of Lothian forms an indivisible part of the Edinburgh land-scape. It is Edinburgh's greatest charm as a city that it *has* a landscape, but from the Pentlands you appreciate how green much of the landscape still is. Thus there are king-fishers at Stockbridge, herons and owls and badgers and foxes deeper inside the city than many of its citizens would believe, and wild swans and greylag geese to set against an urban skyline.

It makes Edinburgh's besieging of the Pentland Hills all the more distressing and disappointing. Of all places, Edinburgh ought to know better.

So the relationship between city and hills has changed, and there is no answering the call of the Pentlands now like Burns or Stevenson, even Reith and Grant, by journeying from the heart of the city, then leaving the city behind, then tramping through a landscape which wilders as it nears the hills. Now the city stops and the hills start, and that transi-tional zone in which you shed the city's yoke and put on the hills' has been shunted back into the hills themselves. In the process, the sense of anticipation which was once such a joy of that journey, has been removed utterly. (In all the Pentlands, it exists now only if you walk into the Cauldstane Slap from Harper Rig – see Chapter 3). You climb Caerketton with the city growling at your heels and the ski-tow creaking in your ear, until you perch above the screes, beneath the

Glencorse and Loganlee reservoirs and the south-west march of the Pentlands' famous skyline – Turnhouse Hill, Carnethy Hill, Scald Law, East Kip, West Kip. Courtesy *Scotsman* Publications.

summit, amid the blaeberries under a tumbledown of ravens, and suddenly the pull of the Pentland Hills has a hold of your sleeve. In a handful of moments, how it all changes!

From the summit of Caerketton, and all the way along the dipping ridge of Allermuir, the Pentlands are revealed as a trailing range of hills lounging away south-west, a cramped airspace of small well-sculpted summits cut by cleuchs and sykes and hopes. These, in the rich vocabulary of the Pentlands, are gorges (sometimes crags), hollows drained by small burns, and steep-sided hill valleys.

One small range of hills, yet there are three subtle variations of landscape which, in the Highlands, would probably be covered by the all-embracing 'glen'. The hill names themselves are often laws or rigs, the laws usually rounded and conical and clearly defined, the rigs being broad-backed ridges (the same old Scots word meant a backbone). It is a substantial legacy of language which the hob-nailed boot of English has tramped into the mire. The extent of the trampling is revealed in such map names as Capelaw Hill and Castlelaw Hill which make as much sense as saying Mount Ben Nevis.

Allermuir's summit throws you an arc of mountains from Ben Lomond to Schiehallion. Pick a sharp winter day when that little cordon of mountainous superstars is a mastercraftsman's white cornice between land and sky and see how many you can name without looking at the summit indicator ... not that that offers too much assistance because much of it is scruffily illegible. It's a scruffy summit in fact, because people who put things on hilltops like direction indicators and stiles and memorials of one kind or another tend to forget that without a commitment to regular protection and maintenance, their creations are wilting under the sustained hostility of their environment. Every day you decide it's too wild to go on the hills, the indicator on Allermuir is being systematically shredded by the weather. A wild hilltop is really no place for anything which doesn't flourish there naturally of its own accord.

The real prize of Allermuir's summit is the view south, where Pentland summits swarm round Glencorse Reservoir and the hills' great landscape cliché disports itself. This is the south-west march of those five summits which are the mental definition of the Pentlands to everyone who knows them intimately – Turnhouse Hill, Carnethy Hill, Scald Law, East Kip, West Kip. They have a kind of snug grandeur about them, clearly defined as mountain individualists, but cunningly designed as an interlocking unit, so that they sometimes look as if they could be picked up as a single landscape component and shifted to another part of the hills, or else unhooked from each other and shuffled, West Kip before East, Scald Law before Turnhouse, that kind of thing. Mountains by Mothercare.

The Logan Valley burrows greenly beneath their west-

The wide sprawl of the Kitchen Moss edges towards the sweep of the Kips with South Black Hill to the right.

ern rampart, dragging down the waters of half a dozen hills and the bulwark of Kitchen Moss into, first, Loganlee Reservoir, then Glencorse. The valley and its barely-broken shoulder-to-shoulder corral of hills ensnares the essence of the Pentland Hills. For the Edinburgh tramper with a day to kill and an old acquaintance to rekindle in his hill-heart, this is what it's all about. No-one can pretend that it is wilderness, and parts of it are not even particularly wild any more, but this small flock of gathered-in hill shapes and outlines still harbours and holds the spirit of the place, the charisma which is unique to the Pentlands, the freedom induced by the scent of hill air, and in my book at least, a sense of that continuity which links the hunting kings of a healthier Scotland, Allan Ramsay and Burns and Scott and Stevenson, Reith and Ogilvie and Grant, and if it comes to that, me. Here I sit and imbibe my own re-distillation of the Pentland wine, a thing of many vintages. I never cross Allermuir without pausing to drink.

There is an older throwback firmly rooted on Allermuir, or rather inside it, for it was in a cleft in the rock near

26

Summer sun on the pale grasses of the East and West Kip and Scald Law, the highest point of the Pentlands. The view is north-east from the flank of East Cairn Hill.

Howden Glen that one R.A. Macfie of Dreghorn unearthed a cache of bones in 1886. Most of the bones were reindeer, although there were also horse, wolf and fox among the hoard. The accepted implication is that here was the lair of a substantial carnivore, although the popular and much regurgitated notion that it was a hyena takes some swallowing. Hyenas do not occur in Scottish historical records, nor do they appear in books like *A Scottish Bestiary,* and a hyena tackling as formidable a fighter as a wolf when there must have been many easier pickings is less than plausible. Yet there is a Boar Stane and a Wolf Craigs in the Pentlands to offer more obvious explanations, and Will Grant suggests that the name Baddinsgill has overtones of bear, without explaining why. Certainly there were brown bears in southern Scotland, well known and much admired by the Romans who sent them home without the hinderance of quarantine legislation or the Wildlife and Countryside Act. So if there was a lair under Allermuir, it was probably a wolf's, and the presence of wolf bones could simply mean a

The opening of the Castlelaw rifle ranges in 1985. The Army presence has dramatically altered the nature of this hill, in what many people feel is quite inappropriate intrusion. Courtesy *Scotsman* Publications.

sick beast died there. Whatever the explanation, the bones are food for thought about where you stand, and the transformed nature of those hills which we are always eager to brand 'unchanging'. Bear, wolf. boar and reindeer inside a regional park, and you thought there was nothing more to worry about than the Army firing range on Castlelaw, or being run over by a mountain bike.

Castlelaw is a sacrificed hill, complete with rifle range, danger zone and a bulldozed road to the summit. The old homily is trotted out routinely to objectors that the Army has to train somewhere, and that, given the proximity of Glencorse Barracks and the containing nature of Castlelaw's south corrie, the Army's purposes can be well served with minimum inconvenience and disturbance to the general public. Every precaution is taken etc., and of course all that is true. But do they have to wreck the best corrie in the Pentlands for all time? Was the bulldozed road really vital for the wellbeing of the national security, or merely convenient (from the summit of Allermuir, the first sensation to confront the eye is not the sprawl of hills but the scar of that road, for its glaring inappropriateness in such a landscape)? Is the Army presence really appropriate, really tolerable, in a landscape of such value? Does its presence within the boundaries of the regional park not demonstrate the futility and the irrelevance of the park?

I have heard it argued, too, that it's only one hill, and we can all enjoy all the other hills, and surely we are not so selfish as to want them all? Apart from the absurdity of the argument, suppose the Army decided to take over a house in the New Town, say, in the middle of Heriot Row, but that for security reasons it had to be reinforced concrete, so the Craigleith sandstone would have to go. But don't worry, it would only be one house and we'd all have the rest of that matchless street to admire. It wouldn't happen, because Edinburgh would see to it that it didn't, but the argument is much the same with Castlelaw and the Pentlands.

As you climb the knobbly shoulder of Turnhouse Hill above Flotterstone, you see what the fuss is all about. You may shudder at the thought of what social historians of the future will make of the remnants of the half-demolished corrie; how would my ghost or yours explain away these historians' bafflement that we let it happen, or what the Army could possibly want with such a place so near the city, and one which the city had earmarked as a regional park because of the charm of its landscape? I think my own ghost would be speechless.

There is evidence of older conflicts on Castlelaw. Today's Army fires live ammunition at non-existent enemies, but two thousand years ago, around the time that the Romans were stamping north up Dere Street, the hill folk of the Pentlands built themselves an oval fort on Castlelaw, and the enemy was anything but invisible. The fort would have had a palisaded enclosure, later a clay and timber rampart, later still ditch ramparts. An earth house was ingeniously burrowed between two ramparts, more likely for storage than for living in. The Romans came and went, and every civilisation since then has washed over or round the patiently enduring fort. We may fume at the presence of the Army and the firing ranges and the rash and dire warning signs like acne on the face of the hill, but it is no more than one more piffling insulting irritant to the fort-builders, the earth-house excavators.

I arrived one day at the Castlelaw car park between the farm and the fort, to find the red flag flying. As I sat in the car readjusting my plans, a soldier appeared and lowered the flag. As it lowered, a brief procession of Army vehicles passed the car park heading into the hills. They were camouflaged, helmeted, armed, serious stuff. But the lowering of the flag meant that the shepherd could unleash his sheep. He opened the gate onto the fort, opened the gate of his sheep pens, and the sheep flowed across the car park unbidden, across the road, through the gate and onto the hill fort, in what is obviously a familiar routine. The convoy, however, had not finished, and the tail end of it just failed to beat the sheep to their crossing point. There is no more immovable object than the flank of an unhurried flock of sheep, so the mock war effort, or whatever, had to wait while the sheep crossed the road. I wondered there and then how many armed convoys on how many roads in how many countries have fumed while a herdsman moved his stock from one piece of ground to another. The warring and the herding are two of the oldest rituals in the history of humanity, and I fancied the watching eyes of the spirits of the hill fort would crinkle in smirking mirth at the warriors who were briefly thwarted by sheep.

The shepherd ushered his last sheep through the gate, waved to the soldiers, and they all went on about their business. I left the car and walked through the sheep to wander the wind-washed ramparts and the snug peace of

The busiest of all the routes into the hills is from the visitor centre at Flotterstone. Here, Turnhouse Hill emerges at a corner of the path.

Loganlee Reservoir and Cartnethy Hill, the very heart of the northern Pentland Hills.

the earth house. In that ancient company, a red flag on a hillside is a terribly flimsy and transient sliver of cloth.

It is a captivating relic, this earth house, even if it has been tidied up a bit for public consumption (glass 'skylights' set into the dome of the hill, plastered upper walls, a heavy iron gate, that kind of thing). The natural curve of the fort's ditch was widened by the earth house builders and lined with a species of drystane dyke into a twenty-yard underground chamber, five or six feet wide. A narrow waist-high passage leads off to a larger and surprisingly high round chamber. The corbelled walls still stand six feet high, but the Department plasterers have taken the walls up to what was presumably their logical conclusion, which is fair enough, I suppose, although the cosmetic nature of the reconstruction is an ill-at-ease hybrid. Still, you see the dimensions of the place as it was, and enough of the building style to know it was the work of considerable craftsmen with an intuitive flair and a sound knowledge of the principles of construction. Which of the twentieth century's hallmarks on the Pentlands can anticipate with any optimism a shelf-life of 2000 years?

A mile across the hill, under a flank of Turnhouse Hill, lies the scene of later conflict, for these Pentland Hills are no strangers to combat or the sight and sound and stench of military operations in all their eras. This time, conflict's hallmark is a single engraved stone. What it commemorates is this:

Rullion Green, November 28, 1666. A ragged gathering, part-army, part-mob, struggles wearily uphill, knowing they are followed, knowing there must be a reckoning. It is why they set out from Galloway after all, or perhaps they are unsure now on this unfamiliar hillside why they set out at all.

They are down to the last nine hundred, cold, tired, dismayed, and knowing that here and now they must turn and face the patient Royalist army of 3000 and more, knowing there is only one outcome, a stone on a hillside.

Yet, are they not Covenanters? The Covenanters who

once made King Charles I eat humble pie, who had worn out Cromwell and seen off the turncoat Montrose, now reduced to guerrilla bands of country folk like this one. Well, not all like this one, for it had done startlingly well at first. It had begun in Galloway, cradled by a raw fury at the brutal work of the King's Commissioners whose policy of collecting taxes from dissenters to the hated episcopacy was often enacted with a sword. From the soldiers' point of view, it enlivened a boring job, and these were, after all, The Killing Times. It was almost expected of them. But the Galloway Covenanters startled the Royalist hit-man Sir James Turner by ignoring the script and capturing him at Dumfries. They flaunted the banners and war slogans of days gone by, and led by a man called Wallace – he would be, wouldn't he? – they recruited a reckless confidence to their first flush of success and set out for Edinburgh. Why? Why not? At their boldest they were 3000-strong. At Lanark, they paused to proclaim loyalty to the King (always a fatal flaw in the Covenanters' campaigns) but demanding the reinstatement of their Presbyterian Kirk, and strict adherence to the National Covenant of 1638 – that which first formalised Scottish resistance to Charles I and his alien church and his ambitions for an absolute monarchy, and which gave the Covenanters their name.

Beyond Lanark, the zeal began to evaporate, desertions whittled away their numbers, the Pentland Hills glowered at their traipsing procession across that dire moorland sprawl, and Edinburgh when they reached it was armed and ready to resist. They turned away, rounding the end of the Pentlands, while Sir Thomas Dalyell of the Binns stalked them coolly, lethally patient. An hour before sunset on November 28, he sent his 600 horse, followed by 3000 disciplined soldiers, and the battle, for want of a better word, was a brief and bloody rout. The Covenanters took to the hills and the night, as they had done and would do so often again.

Rullion Green's prisoners were shown no hint of mercy.

The 2000-year-old hill fort on Castlelaw. An earth house was ingeniously built into the fort's ditched ramparts. The skill of the builders is still evident.

Ten were hanged on one gibbet in Edinburgh, others were taken home and hanged in front of their own folk. Most were deported to Barbados. Some were tortured to death. A few died mercifully quickly on the battlefield.

September 1990. A sheep farm like any other steepens from the West Linton road up the flank of Turnhouse Hill. A shelter belt of pines and beeches, underplanted with young conifers, thwarts the worst of the south-westerly which shrouds the summit in a chilled boil of cloud. The Pentlands are re-asserting themselves after a douce summer. This sheep-spattered field is Rullion Green, just a name on a map – not a place, or a farm, or a house, not even a presence; no sense of history whispers at you from the bracken and the hill grasses. The map also says 'Martyrs Tomb', but omits the wood which all but smothers it, so finding the tomb is no easy task. Mind you, it is the Pentland Hills Regional Park map. But eventually, you find a stone on a hillside.

By now, the stone has been fenced in by an iron railing, painted a bizarre pillar-box red (misguided zeal still seems to cling to this hillside). The stone looks not so much protected as imprisoned, which is a fit enough symbolism, I suppose, even if it wasn't what the fencer hand in mind. But if it was just a stone alone on the moor, washed by wind and rain and time, it would somehow have been better. Now, it looks as though it has backed into the wood, and sheep sharn paves the small corridor between railings and wood. It is a miserable fate for a monument. Discarded fridges and supermarket trolleys fare no worse.

The lettering on the stone fades. This much is discernible: 'Here, and near to this place, lies the Reverend Mr. John Crookshank and Mr Andrew McCormack, ministers of the Gospel, and about fifty other covenanted presbyterians who were killed in this place, in their own innocent self-defence and defence of the covenanted work of reformation by Thomas Dalyell of the Binns upon the 28th of November 1666 ...' Two more lines are indecipherable.

Rullion Green, where a group of Covenanters made their last stand, and gave rise to one the Pentlands' most poignant episodes.

A plaque on the railing reads: 'This plaque, placed here in 1966, at the time of the third centenary of the battle, testifies to the enduring honour accorded to those Covenanters from Galloway and the West who rose in defence of civil and religious liberty. They marched on Edinburgh under the command of Colonel James Wallace, but the time was not ripe and the country failed to support them. On their retreat from the capital, they were overtaken by the Government forces and made their stand on this slope in the late afternoon. About 900 strong and poorly equipped, they faced a trained army of over 3000, After heroic resistance they broke and fled into the winter night.'

It is a cold, crude summary of human torment that a metal plaque inflicts. Better the lonely stone, better too that the stone should be shorn of railing and shelter belt and sheep. Let it stand alone on its hill, guarded by the spirit of those it mourns.

But even this is not the most compelling of the Pentlands monuments to the Covenanters, although considering what happened here, it should be. Ten miles over the hills to the south-west, there was a postcript to Rullion Green which, if anything, says more for the spirit of that broken band of Galloway men than their battlefield courage. We will set that last stone in its due place in this exploration of the Pentland Hills (see Chapter 4).

George Reith, irreverent cocker of snooks that he was, could not resist such a fertile episode, that so-called Pentland Rising which culminated at Rullion Green. There can be few more cynically scathing interpretations of history than this rendering of those events of 1666 in *The Breezy Pentlands:*

'It was the end of a little splutter of rebellion, generally known in history as the Pentland Rising. The name is misleading for though the rebellion was actually crushed at this spot, it broke out in Galloway, where Sir James Turner and his gentle dragoons were endeavouring, by the Christian persuasions of sword and pistol, to convert reluctant Scottish Presbyterians to Episcopacy. The pious Charles II

The Kirk Road and The Green Cleuch meet under Scald Law, 'a vivid little throat of landscape'. Here, too, the Logan Burn leaps down from the Kitchen Moss. '

had declared that Presbyterianism was not fit religion for a gentleman, to which dictum all Presbyterians will heartily subscribe, if Old Rowley himself is to be taken as the moral standard for gentility.

'The policy of his Government was to compel Scottish people to conform to English notions and practices in religion, whether they liked them or not; and military force was added to the ineffectual spiritual persuasions of the curates to further this laudable design. But how slow men are to recognise the benevolent intentions of their superiors! Scotland might by this time have had a religion fit for gentlemen – of a kind – had this Charles of blessed memory been permitted by Providence to have his own way.

' Nothing – not even patriotism – can excuse the obstinacy of the Scotch in refusing to fall in with these plans for their moral and spiritual improvement; and nothing can palliate, in the eyes of the enlightened and cultured historian today [Reith was writing in 1910], the resistance they offered to their King's clerical and military emissaries, no matter how great the provocation they received. Sir James Turner served his royal master with the most praiseworthy zeal, and of course reaped the reward of his fidelity and enthusiasm in the violent dislike of the people of Galloway. One day some of his dragoons in the village of Dalry had stripped an old man and were playfully proceeding to roast him on a red-hot gridiron, for the brutal crime of refusing to attend the ministrations of the episcopal curate in the parish church, and aggravating that crime by declining to pay the fine which the law of the land levied on such refusants. But some peasants overheard the wicked old man's cries, and could not endure the sight of his well-deserved sufferings. The cowardly ruffians deforced the soldiers in the execution of their lawful duties, and made them prisoners ...'

There is much more in this rich vein, but however you tell it, and wherever your sympathies lie, no tramper of the Pentland Hills can cross this hillside, or pass the many secretive folds in the hill where the Covenanters met to

The Martyr's Tomb commemorting the Battle of Rullion Green. The author argues that the stone should be out on the open hill, rather than imprisoned by railings.

worship, fearful of discovery and persecution, without acknowledging a respect for that faith which was honed by the hill winds.

The hill winds of early autumn are the pick of all the Pentlands' airs. The landscape tiredness with which late August always seems to afflict me as well as the hills, yields to the vigour of a new season. The colours of the hills come into their own too, a fast and subtle transformation which depends for its effect both on the muting of summer's worst excesses and the first goldening and reddening of brackens and grasses, sparky heralds of the mature season's unstoppable blaze. Grant noted the change too: 'The clear air of autumn gives the hills a distinctness and nearness that appear preternatural. It almost seems as if we ourselves had changed, so keen is our vision, so light and free our movements, so full of joy our hearts.' Aye, we addicts of autumn, from Keats onwards, were ever given to singing the season's praises, though most of us concede that Keats did it better than the rest of us.

September is the headiest distillation of the old and new, and if your journey tramps those patched heather acres of grouse moor, the colour-questing can be a kaleidoscopic richness. Sunlight is not necessary, in fact it is not even preferable, for on the dullest days, the hills provide _all_ the colour, and the subtleties grow more perceptible.

This first came home to me on a day of thudding winds which turned a light rain into a persistent stinging of my left cheek, an effect achieved by the wind delivering the rain sideways and at about 60 miles an hour. I had chosen the Kirk Road, over the pass between Scald Law and Carnethy and down as far as that vivid little throat of a landscape at the entrance to the Green Cleuch, then wheeling away southwest with the Logan Burn up onto the Kitchen Moss, and back to the Kirk Road over the Kips and Scald Law. Every shade and every Pentlands landform and waterform crops up somewhere on such a trek, but I always find a pause by the gate under Scald Law irresistible, even with less than half a mile at my back. It seems that beyond the dyke you are embraced by the hills, and that before it, you are quite outwith the hills. It is a psychological transition but a very profound one, and quite the antithesis in terms of joining the fellowship of the hills to the long seductive moorland insinuations of Cauldstane Slap from Harper Rig.

There is a protective, almost possessive, feel about the hills here where the Kirk Road cuts snugly through heather and bracken and clambers a green cleft to 1456 feet, almost 600 feet above the road, and 500 feet above the Logan Valley on the other side. Over this pass, the people of the Logan Valley used to trek to church in Penicuik and back every Sunday ... call it six miles there and back with a total ascent and descent of 2200 feet, or eight miles if you happened to live a mile away from the Howe on the Logan side of the pass.

I watched a party of walkers trailing down the green slope ahead and translated them in my mind's eye into the black-and-grey Sabbath procession of the valley folk, trying to fathom the significance to them of such a ritual. What went through their minds when the minister led them into 'I to the hills will lift mine eyes'? Was the journey a joy or a penance? Were they battlers through snows and floods, or were they inclined to skip it at the least excuse? I suspect the former – and that their fitness and their stoicism and their faith must have been formidable.

My eyes wandered from the path to the hills. From here, it is Carnethy, not Scald Law, which looks the more impressive hill mass, and the richer by far in its colours. I found six distinct shades in the heather alone – the full flowering of the pale ling, the ecclesiastical purple of the bell heather, the sporadic splash of white flowers, and three phases of withering which showed as a bright foxy brown, a duller brown, and a greeny-black where the thickest of the bell heather had withered. The bracken was still a green sea, but gold was on the curving tips of the highest leaves, the breaking waves of autumn. The beauties of its death throes are bracken's only saving graces. The brightest splashes on the hill are the short grass of the sykes, and these seem to grow more vivid as summer recedes. The duller the day, the greener they glow, the giddier the contrast with the pink screes. Only nature would dare emerald and pink together, and expect to get away with it.

The Howe at the head of Loganlee Reservoir adds trees to the spill of colour and textures, but on such a day, the watersheet itself is too wind-perplexed to contribute new shades. But catch it on a still day, and see how the water emphasises the patterns in the landscape, for all that its reflection is blurred and darkened and its colours softened. At the Howe, too, you have re-entered that central atrium of the Pentlands which reaches from Glencorse Reservoir to Kitchen Moss, and which, at this end, is as wild and secretive as the Flotterstone end is tamed and open-armed.

From Flotterstone you wander (or drive if you are one of the privileged few) the metalled road to Glencorse where the drowned remnants of the chapel of St. Katherine's-in-the-Hopes slumber away their oblivion between droughts. One of the less credible stories of the Pentlands has it that the chapel was built by one William St. Clair, ancestor of the Earls of Rosslyn, as a result of an unlikely wager with his hunting companion, King Robert the Bruce no less. The pair had put up a white deer, and the reckless St. Clair wagered his head against a tract of the royal hunting estate that his hounds would bring down the deer before it crossed the Logan Burn. If the story is true, these two were either remarkably good friends, or remarkably good enemies, for the Bruce is alleged to have accepted the wager, and dutifully paid up when he lost it. St. Clair's second reckless gesture of the day was to immortalise the hour and the King's generosity – not to mention astounding sportsman-ship – by building a chapel on the spot.

He reckoned without the contempt for mediaeval wagers which is built into the bureaucratic fabric of water authorities the length and breadth of the land.

From the Kirk Road, however, the valley of the Logan Burn is rather more the Pentlands the Bruce might recognise, The Kirk Road, the Green Cleuch, the burn of the Lover's Loup, and the Logan Burn fresh from the high moor all gather at a magical transforming crossroads of landscapes. Take any one of those routes and the landscape changes at once from the one you have just left. It is the kind of place, too, where on a day of tumbling mists you might expect an encounter with a spectral band of moss-troopers or a furtive gathering of Covenanters, or the ghost of Stevenson stepping jauntily through the bouldery land. If you hold with the idea of an immortal soul, surely Stevenson's roams these hills.

The beaten path is a green swirl through the Green Cleuch. The unbeaten one, which I now chose, slips narrowly into a small den where dippers nest by the Logan Burn's only serious attempt at a waterfall. The charm of the Pentland Hills is largely a subtle affair, but here it is a startling jewel hoarded away in an open casket of the hills, its presence quite unsuspected and utterly hidden from fifty yards away in any direction. Once you pass the fall, turn and look back, and you see only the implied depths of that landscape crossroads in its valley, the baulking wall of Black Hill, the wrap-round summits of Carnethy and Turnhouse Hill.

A fickle species of track navigates through the Kitchen Moss's lower reaches, and lures you into another and utterly different hill world. There are no hiding places from the wind on the high mosses of the Pentlands, and it blew that September afternoon with an elemental rawness giving the flimsy rain an edge as hard as buckshot. I endured an interminable head-down mile of it in which no living thing moved which wasn't a sheep, and I grew heartily sick of the colour purple. But such lapses are brief and forgiveable (the psychology of even such meek hills as these can be a formidable foe as well as a hand-in-glove companion – the trick is to try and immerse yourself in the hills' mood and match it. Experience teaches the trick, that and a willingness to become as much a fragment of the landscape as is humanly possible. It is less likely that you will succeed in a purple anorak and a pink rucksack. Try dirty green.)

No matter that this landscape has more grid-iron horizontals than a *Scotsman* crossword puzzle (the result of zealous drainage ditching), the Moss is a reservoir of many wildnesses. I caught myself reincarnating those May mornings which are anthems to the tribes of moorland birds. If you can lock that music into your mind, that too can help to restore your flagging faith on the ungolden days.

There is another wildness in the scope of the Moss. If you have worked your way from Flotterstone or Allermuir, you have graduated from the close-knit and confiding landscape of the clear-cut northern Pentlands to the open-palmed places. The Kitchen Moss is a watershed of landscapes and it is worth pausing in its airy midst to see how the hills close ranks tidily at your back, setting everything into place, but sprawl indistinctly ahead. The south-west shore of that high moor is a low-slung shoal of whaleback summits, those far spreadeagled hill shapes which characterise the Pentlands beyond the unseen Cauldstane Slap.

A signpost appeared high on a corner of the skyline, two hundred yards away, marking the line of another cross-Pentlands route from Nine Mile Burn to Balerno via the Monks Road (ecclesiastical references and allusions are irresistible in the Pentlands). I dislike these signs, and for all the diligence of the Scottish Rights of Way Society and others who champion the cause of these ancient routes, a tall metal sign is an incongruous irritant, a deliberately implanted wart on the face of the moor. If such routes must be signposted, why not mark them with low milestones, using real stone? The Pentlands paths are so well defined (and it must be said such delightful walking that you could enjoy a rich lifetime without leaving them) that surely it needs no more than a rudimentary knowledge of map-reading and a little familiarity with the ground to navigate their network. We don't need signs too, or the park's wretched yellow arrows.

It is hardly a new practice in the Pentlands, this route-marking with posts, and the oldest paths are marked in places by a species of venerable ancients like lopped-off telegraph poles. These were the work of what was then The Scottish Rights of Way and Recreation Society Limited, Edinburgh. They have at least the merit of weathering, while their modern counterparts simply rust, but they are just as ugly and just as unnecessary, even though some of them are a hundred years old. The sixpenny booklet *The Pentland Hills Their Paths and Passes (with a map)* produced for the society in 1885, neatly confounds itself with its description of the start of the Cauldstane Slap, thus: 'A direction board has been erected by the Rights of Way Society at this point, and it is much needed, for there are hardly any traces of a road now down the dyke-side. However, proceed in faith, and noting the instructions on the direction board to "keep to the line of the posts" we start straight away for the head of the Pass which is plainly before us all the way, with the rocky summits of the Cairn Hills on either side of it ...'

But if the head of the pass is 'plainly before us all the way', why are the direction board and the line of posts necessary to get there?

The remarkable thing about this little centenarian of a booklet is that the Society's tone is just as twee and insistent now as it was then. If the true national tradition of Scotland is freedom to roam – and it is – then rights of way are irrelevant, and the case for their preservation little more then the case for preserving any artefact of history.

To be sure, some of them have wondrous histories, and the Pentlands would be the poorer without them, but they should play no part in any argument about access to the hills, for if freedom to roam is accompanied by responsibility and respect for the land and those who work it, then the Scot on his native heath should be an unfettered animal.

I turned away from the signpost high on the Kitchen Moss, having admired the art of the nearby dyke which it so demeans. The one is wrought from the rock of the hills and lives and breathes with the hills. The other is carelessly prefabricated and plonked in the ground to be as conspicuous and alien as possible. The path it serves, however, is a beauty, and this highest stretch the very best of it. The relief of putting the sting of the rain onto the other side of my face was another blessing of the new direction of my route. Blessings come in all disguises on the Moss.

By the time the path reaches the 1500-feet contour, it is high on a shoulder of West Kip, and there yet another pole serves as a miniature roundabout, a junction of four routes. Three of them, admittedly, descend to the West Linton road, and two of the three to Nine Mile Burn. The fourth climbs the switchbacks of the Kips and Scald Law, and Carnethy and Turnhouse too, if you feel inclined. The southmost of the four is the Monks Road which skirts a stuttering, wind-smashed wood and curves over Gap Law and Monks Rig and into another episode of the hills story.

The route was one which monks followed for centuries between the monastery at Newhall near Carlops and Dunfermline (via Queensferry). A small piece of shaped rock lies at the side of the track where it contours Monks Rig, and although it is called the Font Stane today, there is little doubt that it once acted as a socket for a stone cross. Why there, and what function it served is long forgotten, but like all the road's travellers both Reith and Grant found it irresistible. Reith, with a little help from his constant friend *Brown's Notes on Penicuik,* and an 1808 edition of Allan Ramsay's *The Gentle Shepherd,* averred that 'it formed part of some larger structure, for it is described as a stone trough in its middle, two excavations on its side as if for a person's knees, and a socket at its end for a cross.' Both Ramsay's book and Brown's noted that the head of the cross ('ornamented', says Brown) still lay at the foot of the Rig. The stone, according to Reith, writing in 1910, 'scarcely

The Font Stane on the Monks Road high above Nine Mile Burn. It almost certainly was the base of a stone cross at one time, but its purpose remains another Pentlands mystery.

corresponds to the description now; time and weather have worn it thin and shallow.' The cross, he added, had 'wholly disappeared'.

Grant adds a wealth of detail, but no explanation. It is, he says, 'a block of Silurian grit 3 feet by 2 feet 8 inches, and 10-15 inches high, lying due north and south, having a cavity in the middle 20 inches by 12 inches and 9 inches deep, with two indentations on the wide eastern edge, perhaps meant for the knees of the worshipper at a cross, which originally stood in the centre ...'

'Whether it was a Font Stone, a wayside shrine, or a landmark commanding all the country to the south for the pious friar as he journeyed over the hills .... who can tell? But there it remains today, and as we stand and meditate upon it, we link ourselves with a visible symbol of the time when the white robed monk was a familiar figure in the Pentland Hills.'

That is the real worth of these old Pentland paths, apart from the intrinsic pleasure of just being on them. It is that sense of tramping history's imprint. You thread the same route which was fashioned by the feet of the workaday world as it trampled its story into the Pentlands soil, oblivious to the fascination with which eras like ours would scrutinise its tread. The same hill shapes would mark its progress across the landscape and it would feel the raw edge of the same wind, take refuge in the lee of the same rocks and craigs and hopes and hollows. The monks, the drovers, and all the other travellers – whatever their motives – who stamped those ancient routes onto the face of the Pentland Hills through every century before this one would understand more of the hills than we do. These were matter-of-fact roads to them, not day excursions, that fox-straight shortest distance between two points. To work the hills was to live. Whether we now brand these routes as 'rights of way' or not changes none of that, although it is arguable that it may safeguard some of it. But an old stone lying by a wayside with a socket in it for a cross will survive and tell its own story of its own accord, but only if we inheritors of the Monks Road pause respectfully, then pass on and leave it be.

But Grant also records a second such stone which lay between Scald Law and the South Black Hill, and speculates that it may be found in a nearby drystane dyke. I looked, but didn't find, but I like that idea – the stone which held the cross of the Good Shepherd helping to keep the truculent Pentlands flocks in check.

All through that day of September storm which had begun with the colour-collecting on the Kirk Road, one shade and shape glowered over the proceedings. From the highest point of the Kitchen Moss track where it gathers four ways together under West Kip, that shape and its shade are at their most sinister. As a rule, I don't hold with the notion that hills as individuals can be 'sinister' or 'black' or otherwise ill-at-ease with their fellows, but Black Hill with the livid weal of its bulldozed road is the Pentlands' exception to my own rule. It was well named by the hill folk, and the greyer the day, the blacker its mood. It is a curiosity of the Pentlands that from almost any angle and at any season, that fivefold regime of hills from the Kips to Turnhouse is a pale hierarchy clad in the lightest of hill grasses. Just as the greyest day darkens Black Hill's blackness, so it pales the hills across the valley of the Logan Burn. I fancy them as ancient rivals, Scald Law and its attendants ranged against the huge mass of Black Hill, white knight and black, ancient combatants in an unresolved conflict. Or perhaps they are petrified mythological figures like Am Bodach and A'Chailleach, the Old Man and the Old Woman of much legend who glower at each other across Gleann Einich in the Cairngorms.

I have come across no such legend in the Pentlands, however. Perhaps now is the time to invent one, and slip it surreptitiously into these pages as authenticated folklore with a pedigree centuries old? I wouldn't be the first. I settle instead for a flight of fancy lent a certain credibility by the heightened colourations of that flattened light. But heather-

dark Black Hill with the hideous scar on its brow and scalp
has yet to win my affections.

It was a flattening wind which thrust me up and over the
Kips, so strong that it was almost impossible to stand still
going uphill. All the plantations under the Kips, and all the
way down to the road, bear the hallmarks of such winds. The
Pentlands may not be arduous hills, nor even particularly
wet ones, but they do magnetise the winds. They thrust me
over Scald Law whose summit pays the price of being the
highest. Nobody who walks the Pentlands doesn't want to
climb Scald Law, and for all its modest 1899 feet, it is a
fittingly fetching summit, small and shapely and throwing
you a staggering swathe of Scotland for your trouble, especially if you happen to catch it all with the air at its
crystalline best. In terms of what we used to call counties,
you can see to one extent or another East, Mid and West
Lothian, Fife, Kinross, Clackmannan, Perth, Angus, Stirling,
Lanark, Argyll, Roxburgh, Selkirk, Peebles and Berwick,
and I wouldn't argue with those who stake claim for slivers
or skyline bumps of Dumfries, Ayr, Renfrew, and old-
fashioned detached Dumbarton. The problem is the kind
of day to test the theory, although it is perhaps less of a
problem now than George Reith found it:

'The difficulty is to get a perfectly clear day ... there is
always cloud, mist, or haze about somewhere [Auld Reekie
would still be reeking filthily at the time] and to the north-
west the chimneys of the oil country and of the iron works
about Falkirk not only pollute the atmosphere in their
immediate neighbourhood but obscure the view in that
direction. Which is trying to those who are not shareholders
in either oil or iron companies.'

I wonder what he would have made of Grangemouth.

It is a fast jaunt down the wide and spreading erosion of
Scald Law's summit slopes to the Kirk Road again; I stopped
at the gate in the dyke where you step in and out of the hills.
On such a day, there must have been many a muddy boot
traipsed into the Penicuik kirks, and many a good suit

scented with sharn. Most of us go to the Pentlands for the fun of it, or for what they offer us as a restorative, or just to keep their company or watch their wildlife; a few more of us live and work in them; none of us knows, or can even imagine, how it was when the Kirk Road led to and from the Kirk.

The Heartland Hills

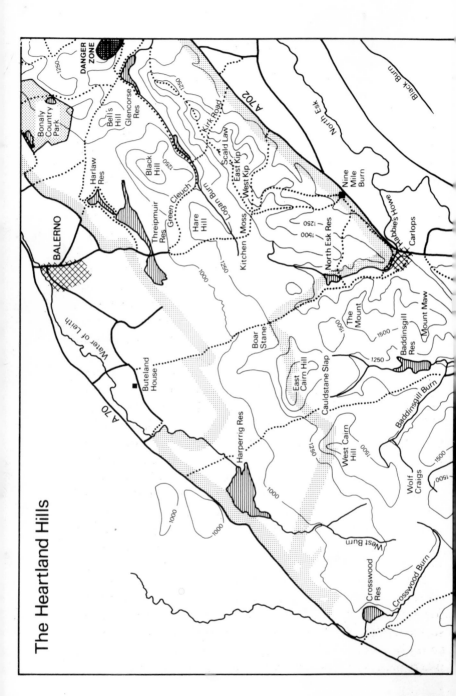

CHAPTER 3

The Heartland Hills

In the early years of the fourteenth century, Edinburgh was still a walled-in rock. Scotland was not so much a nation as an uneasy coalition of factions (some things never change), and The Bruce was watching spiders. But the Cauldstane Slap was already a highway – 'the high road of the cairns' – an integral and infamous part of the route between Highlands and Lowlands, an eight-mile hill pass which bisects the Pentlands with a disconcerting way of confounding navigation – this because although it connects the west side of the range with the east, and has an east-west feel about it, it actually runs more or less north-north-west to south-south-east. Matters are not helped by the fact that East Cairn Hill is more obviously north of West Cairn Hill than east of it.

There are other confusions. Why Cauldstane? Why Slap? To be sure it can be gey cauld. To be sure there are stanes, great heaps of them on the summits of East and West Cairn Hills which guard its northern end, but the whole is neither caulder nor staneyer than the rest of the hills. Grant, always eager to enlighten, is conspicuously silent. Reith fences doubtfully and concedes: 'The origin of Cauldstane I have been unable to ascertain.' He's convincing enough on Slap, though: 'Slap means a permanent opening in a dyke through which sheep or cattle may pass with no gate attached. A gate that lies open, however, may be in the slap. It is here used figuratively to describe this narrow pass in the hills.'

Through which, he might have added, cattle and sheep passed for four centuries and more along one of Scotland's foremost drove roads. A good Scottish dictionary lends support to the gap idea, and adds simply 'a pass or shallow valley between hills' and suggests it was used frequently in place names in east and west central Scotland from the

Midwinter on East and West Cairn Hill, guardians of the Cauldstane Slap. The Slap is the most famous and infamous of all the Pentlands' passes.

eighteenth century on. The date is corroborated by two earlier map references to 'Coldstounstopp' and 'Colstounslope'.

The Colstounslope intrigues – simply the slope above the coal toun that was some long-forgotten mining community at one end of the pass? Or how about this? Bearing in mind that it was traipsed for centuries by Highland drovers, its origin may be not Scots but Gaelic, not Cauldstane or Colstoun but Coiltean, meaning woods. Both ends of today's pass still have woods, even the Harper Rig end, where the trees are notably conspicuous on a stretch of country famous for its treelessness. Four or five hundred years ago there would have been woods. So the name could be one of these hybrids of Gaelic and Scots which are everywhere in our landscape. It is a good game, whatever the long-lost truth of it.

The hills look far off from Harper Rig, defensive and coy. The mile-wide moorland shelf which lies before you is a douce deception for an introduction to such as the

56

'East Cairn Hill is a low slouch, dipping undramatically towards the summit of the pass.' Moss Troopers and cattle rustlers would know its outline well.

Cauldstane Slap. All that is infamous about the Slap is unguessable from here.

This late-August balm – warm winds and high clouds which patch hill and moor with fast suns and shadows, the landscape giddily ripe in purple and violent green – it is hardly the stuff of the Thieves' Road of historic infamy, so dreaded by centuries of drovers. Moss troopers and rustlers *here?* Secret coteries of Covenanters stashed away amid the rocks – here? It's all too poised, too purply pristine for that. East Cairn Hill is a low slouch, dipping undramatically towards the summit of the pass. West Cairn Hill is just a distant shrug. The pass itself is as unlike a pass as you can imagine. The only predatory influences in sight are flying. Three kestrels slide down the hill air working the moor in loose formation, fifty yards between birds, methodical as grouse beaters. One by one they wheel into the wind and pause, head-down, fan-tailed, expectant, stitched to the air. One by one they flick out of that wind-hovering trance and

The 'amiable companionship' of a drystane dyke is an unmistakeable guide to the summit of the Cauldstane Slap from Harper Rig, and the haunt of countless small birds.

fly on, turning again to stop and stare. It is a mesmeric routine. The glasses show that the middle bird is the youngster, so it's possibly a training flight. Watch, wait, follow. The nearest bird falls, flattens, falls, flattens, falls, hits the plum-purple moor, the soft thud of landing carrying clearly across the wind. A frantic squeak is just audible, just as brief. The bird rises, cuts low and slow across the moor, a warm and limp vole slung beneath it like an undercarriage. The two other kestrels fly patiently on.

Good. Blood and murder! Now we're getting somewhere. This is more like the Cauldstane Slap of yore. Quicken the step, away with this moorland dawdling. Bring on the moss troopers!

'The name Cauldstane Slap has an eerie sough in the sound of it,' wrote Grant, 'and it was an eerie place, whether in the black darkness of a winter night and the howling of the storm when the cruel north wind was tearing through the Slap, or on a still night of fitful moonlight, and woe betide the drover and his herd that were resting there when upon the wings of the wind came the thudding of horses' hoofs and the jingling of spurs and bridles.'

So you make what eeriness and soughs you can out of your August morning and tramp up towards the skyline where the unseen pass dips into the very heartland hills of the Pentlands, and where, more than anywhere else in all the hill miles from Hillend to Kaimend, the hills swarm round and shutter the world beyond. The reincarnation of the drovers' frame of mind does not come easily. Today's track is another right of way and suffers from the ugly signatures of the Pentland Hills Regional Park – a rash of yellow way markers and other stick-to-the-path insinuations. Console yourself that with a few thousand head of cattle trampling more or less the same line, a few thousand more sheep making the reverse journey from the market at West Linton to the north, the track is a lot less of a mire – and a lot more fragrant – than it once was.

It doesn't alter the fact that it's worse than it needs to be, and the park's territorial declaration of this its southern boundary is as pointless as it is irritating. The implication of it all is that you are incapable of plotting what is a blatant route across a few hundred yards of in-bye farmland and threading your way to the summit of the Slap up a moorland slope bisected by a dye-straight drystane dyke which itself reaches the skyline within a few yards of the summit cairn. It's the kind of thing which happens when hills are managed by half-baked theories about leisure pursuits from city offices.

I divert my own prejudices away from the path and tramp uphill with the amiable companionship of the dyke. This one is a right of way, too, for scores of small birds – wheatears, whinchats, finches, wrens, once (incomprehensibly) a green woodpecker with no wood nearer to peck than a waymarker post – and roughly paved with a thick fur of lichen. A brood or two of wheatears tumbles up the dyke before me, in every shade of plumage from the off-white straggles of the fledglings to the blue-grey and white and black and ochre of the adult males. All of them flash a white postscript as they leap to snatch insects and fall back to the dyke. The formal explanation of the bird's name is that it is from two Anglo-Saxon words – 'hwit' meaning white and 'oers' meaning rump – but I much prefer the colloquially presentable explanation that it is a prissy Victorian clean-up of the rural Scottish 'white-arse'. The birds themselves don't much care one way or the other, but they are energetic and charming company through the Pentland springs and summers, and the dykes and the moors and the hill-folk miss them through the winter. It is always a good March day which coughs up the first rattling wheeze of the new migrants, the first flourish on a rock above the Slap of a blithe white arse.

The wrens skip among them as they wander the ridge of the dyke, but whereas the wheatears tend to treat the dyke as a stationary aircraft carrier, the wrens plunder the dyke itself for its rich and minute community of creeping crawling things such as a wren likes to get its metaphorical teeth into.

High on the dyke, the dozen or so freewheeling birds which have climbed ahead of me for the last half-hour suddenly scatter wide as buckshot and fly far down the moor in a unanimous panic. The source of their discomfort is a tiny gleaming ripple of chestnut which suddenly catches my drift, and in the insatiable manner of all the weasel tribe, vents its curiosity on my presence. This it does by standing on hind legs on a stone perch half-a-weasel-wide, and boring into me with fearless black eyes. Another thing the dyke is good for is weasels, and their stoat cousins, for they use it as a highway to spring along, a maze to hide or sleep in or play in or hunt in, which is all quite a compliment to something so blatantly man-made.

Mosses and moths like dykes too. So does anything the length and breadth of the hills which has cause to perch or pause or squirm or squeak or seek out the nooks and niches and crannies which offer the solaces of survival to the lesser living things of the hills. I like dykes. This one lures you as far as the watershed, after which it right-turns south-west and slidders away up West Cairn Hill. Whether you are for the hill or the pass, the pause to admire the newly revealed interior of the hills is irresistible. The hills around the Slap are an interlocking intrigue of suggestive curves, defined and slashed by burns and sykes and cleuchs, punctuated with blunt thrusts of rock – White Craigs, Cloven Craig, and a surprisingly anonymous rock rough-and-tumble high on a flank of East Cairn Hill. The Kips crop up far over the shoulder of Wether Law, end-on now, mountainously different from their brother hills. The track of the Cauldstane Slap becomes wider, sharper-defined and suddenly ensnared. For all the day's August cheer, there is a fey presence about the land beyond the summit, as though something irretrievable has been sealed behind you when you pass between the Cairn Hills.

I was so struck with the sensation the first time I ever crested the pass at the fag-end of a drab and drookit winter that I now tested it out purposefully on the height of summer. It held good. My theory runs that the hills seem to inhale you with an imperceptible and sustained breath; they encroach on your passage so subtly that before you are aware of it, they have barred the landscape at your back and shut out those elements of the land which imply all we associate with the freedom of the hills – breadth, space, far horizons, silence. In their place have been planted hill walls, shadows, secrecies, whispers.

These were what surely turned the drovers' heads, not just for their implicit danger but also because it followed so hard on the heels of the moorland miles and wide horizons at their back, and because the transition was such a deception. It was almost as if the hills themselves were a part of the conspiracy.

No matter how often I have tried, I cannot surprise the hills into not surprising me. Now, of course, the psychology of it has a double edge, and I anticipate not the absence of the surprise but the fact of it, and still it doesn't fail. The drovers, who lived the landscape and must have been able to read it much as we might read a street map, who crossed the Slap many times thrusting their black beasts forward, would know a more penetrating anticipation, translate it perhaps as fear, perhaps as challenge, for they were made of stern stuff themselves and moulded by harder mountain lands than these. Stevenson gave them this character reference: 'The drove roads lay apart from habitation; the drovers met in the wilderness as today the deep-sea fishermen meet off the banks in the solitude of the Atlantic, and in the one as in the other case rough habits and fist-law were the rule. Crimes were committed, sheep filched, and drovers robbed and beaten; most of which offences had a moorland burial and were never heard of in the courts of justice.'

It all begs the question – why? Why court such danger in such places? Why not avoid them? Go round the hills? The answer is twofold. One that the drovers were hillmen themselves, born to it and at one with it. It would always be their natural environment. The other is that it was better for the cattle, and there was no higher priority for the drover than what was best for the cattle. 'He avoided the highways which distressed the bullocks' feet,' wrote Grant, 'and the turnpike annoyed his freedom-loving spirit. He knew the necessity of bringing his beasts to market in good condition and free from leg-weariness; the green places where feeding was obtainable, and the resting places where there was water, were as well known to him as the places where danger lurked.'

I followed the dyke up West Cairn Hill. A month ago I had stood near the summit amid a swarm of cloudberry, startling and pink, and far from the most common fruits of the hill in Scotland. I cursed the absence of a camera. Today I had one, and the cloudberry leaves were crimson and shrivelled and finished. There was not a berry on the face of the hill. Blaeberry and crowberry were burgeoning crops amid the heather, mile after mile of them, but in the small

An old sheep fold nestles on a broad shelf above the small valley of the Baddinsgill Burn. A dilapidated wood haunts the skyline.

and densely populated cloudberry communities, there were only ankle-high ghost towns.

From West Cairn Hill, you win back those far horizons you sacrifice on the crest of the Cauldstane Slap. The surprise is finding things in places where you don't expect them, another consequence of the confusing slants of the Pentland Hills themselves and the line of the Slap.

The Forth Bridge leaps hugely from its landscape, its scale somehow magnified by distance, but far to the left of where you might expect to find it. The whole chain of peaks of the southern Highlands is likewise shunted across the landscape – Ben Lawers, Ben Chonzie, Ben Vorlich, Stuc a' Chroin, Ben More, Stobinian, Ben Ledi, Ben Venue, Ben Lomond ... a handsomely sequenced frontier to that greater landscape beyond the Forth. The drovers crossed that too. Schiehallion stands solitary and heroic, the way it always seems to in any light and from any direction. Limitless Border hills peel off south-west, and the southern Pentlands bound away to Dunsyre and the bold bulwark of the Moorfoots.

The Baddinsgill Burn 'is a well-flowered jaunt on an August afternoon, starred with eyebright and bog-asphodel and bog-cotton and harebell and ragged robin and field scabious and swarms of tormentil and bedstraw'.

The low ground is less appealing. Razor-edged conifer plantations of spellbinding dullness advance on these south-west Pentland slopes with all the ominous intent of Birnam Wood bearing down on Macbeth. Regrettably this is the shape and dreary shade of things to come west of the Pentlands, and further encroachments seem inevitable. It is all the more sad that almost all the hills' old woods, whether natural or planted, are in more or less terminal decline. There is always money to fence in the huge commercial plantations. There is rarely money, or the will, or both, to fence in the small delightful woods of places like Baddinsgill Burn or the summit of Monks Rig. It is an old equation which makes no sense – the woods provide shelter for sheep, and sheep bring death to the woods by grazing away any prospect of natural regeneration. Oh, the woods won't die in our lifetimes, not completely, but our children or theirs will see most of them out.

I held to the high ground of West Cairn Hill only as far as its southern cairn, then dipped away down into the valley of

Hoolet's Hoose by Loganlee Reservoir, so called, according to Will Grant, "by the local folks centuries ago as being the habitation of owls".

the Baddinsgill Burn, eyeing the tip of the pinewood which holds hard to the Whauplie Rig. It's a rich and thoughtful tongue, the lowland Scots, and it takes a dull soul not to relish the sound of 'Whauplie Rig' and turn the appropriateness of it over on his tongue, and speak it into the hill air. I hold such as Torweaving Hill and Mealowther and Black Birn and Deerhope Rig and Hoolets Hoose and Baron's Cleuch just as fondly for the sound of them, for the way they read on the map, and for the way they jell with the land.

The burn that saunters under the Whauplie Rig is a well-flowered jaunt on an August afternoon, starred with eyebright and bog-asphodel and bog-cotton and harebell and ragged robin and field scabious and swarms of tormentil and bedstraw. Forget-me-nots linger on and some of the foxgloves in the bracken are startling white. Stonechats, dapper-capped, perch on the fronds and sway with them, their calls cracking on the air like live wires. Long before the pinewood re-emerges round a hidden bend of the burn, there is a new screeching voice to challenge the stonechats and drown out the muttering burn. It's a familiar refrain of the wild woods, and it means sparrowhawks.

So I hugged the far side of the burn and found a perch on a hill shoulder to watch the wood. The sparrowhawks were a family of four, the parent birds still fetching and carrying for the newly-feldged young, and every fetch and carry was greeted with the same raucous chorus. Every brief wing-flexing flight of the young birds also culminated in the same screech. It sounds like the most vicious-tongued of harangues. In practice it is simply a way of staying in touch, like a handshake or a hug. The sparrowhawks' deft flight through trees has always captivated me, and here were rank novices and master craftsman in eloquent demonstration of the fundamental truth that even a sparrowhawk must hone his art.

In fact there were four degrees of that art on display. At its peak, the adult male, being the smaller of the pair, was

Mountain bikers in the Cauldstane Slap, a jarring presence. 'Mountain bikes quite literally ride roughshod over the simplicity of the hills'.

lethally efficient and fearless even in the tightest, twiggiest spaces. You would think there was no more confident realm for the smaller woodland birds than these lacy traceries of twigs and small branches and pine fronds, but when there are sparrowhawks in residence, few pursuits are fruitless. The adult female is a heavier-set bird, and (it seems to me) less agile in the tightest corners of the wood. Of the youngsters, one was so ungainly as to be fresh from the nursery, the shortest flight a thing of endless obstacles and treacheries, not easily eluded. The other had obviously had a headstart in terms of flying hours, traipsing from branch to limb and upturned root and back to branch with unsubtle certainty. The turn of speed would be next, the thrill of the first chase, the puff of feathers at the first yellow-footed strike still the stuff of dreams.

The land was slumbrous and still over the hill where Hareshaw Syke sclaffs down a few hundred yards of bog to the Baddinsgill Reservoir. The burn seemed to be all that moved. The wind that had bounced cloud shadows across the morning hills was suddenly silent. In the absence of that driving force, the clouds log-jammed into a spreading gray canopy, and held the afternoon in uneasy warmth.

It is a trick I have developed over the years of wandering Scotland's hills that when I encountered a particular landscape in a particularly intense mood, I try and conjure in my mind's eye the antithesis of that mood. Thus, as I swilled Pentland water and scoffed chunks of apple, bread and cheese, I set my mind on an old day of mid-March with late snow on the tops and Baddinsgill awash with the snow-melt and the new invasion of whaups and peesies – curlews and lapwings to those who haven't yet mastered the language of the Pentlands. It was one of those days when the balance of old season and new was on a knife-edge, and about to be tipped irrevocably springwards. It is the headiest hill day of all when you trudge up out of winter's old doldrums and hear the first drooling curlew cry, the first giddy lapwing whoop, crying on the wind of the Slap. Then you pass the gate above the reservoir and step onto the open hill to find the air and the moor and the hill ringing with their flights and voices, their feet deaved by the sprinting darts of ringed plovers. The only rival to such a day is that November hour when the first brass bands of whooper swans come bulging over the Lang Whang, homing in on Bavelaw, winter's herald birds.

So I sit on a stuffy day of August and juggle seasons in my mind, wondering at the patience of the hills as the sounds and strains of all seasons and all years spread and ripen and wither and fade. In such a frame of mind you can contemplate the brief reign of the Pentland Hills in terms of the history of the planet, and wonder what eternity feels like.

I took the Slap as far as White Craigs (I haul up onto these rocks like a seal on a skerry, my favourite perch in all the Pentlands for seeing and thinking and feeling, for it seems to lie in the midst of a definitive cross-section of the hills). I was for crossing the Thieves' Road and tramping over to

East Cairn Hill when my solitary day was gatecrashed by the late twentieth-century's equivalent of moss troopers, the scourge of the Cauldstane Slap, the breachers of hill peace. You find them increasingly in wilder and wilder places, oblivious to the sanctity of footfall and bird cry and deer bark. Civilised man has turned his hands to few more tormenting inventions than these. Mountain bikes.

I realise that it is hard to make a case against the passage across the hills of a few bikes when the pedigree of that particular swathe of hills is as a thoroughfare for thousands of head of cattle, horsemen, and all manner of foot travellers from monks and tramps to James IV and Mary Queen of Scots, but they must be seen in the context of today's hills. The great majority of people who go on the hill today do so for what the hill has to offer – wildness, silence, space, peace, wildlife, geology, spiritual respite, some of these or all of them.

Just being among the hills is enough for many. But mountain bikes tend to be there for shallower motives. They are gaudy and travel in spaced-out convoys so that communication demands shouting. They are brash and intrusive and they make a hell of a mess. The object of the exercise is to give the undoubted rough-terrain capabilities of the bikes a thorough work-out. That means exploring the wildest of the hills, and it means overwhelming the peace of those who pursue those simpler pleasures which demand the simplicity of the hills. Mountain bikes quite literally ride roughshod over the simplicity of the hills.

Yet – and there is one more crass gesture by the bureaucrats – the Pentland Hills Regional Park sees fit to accommodate them specifically within its realm, and issues a kind of highway code with its walking map of the Pentlands. That code reads 'Mountain biking is recognised as a legitimate use of public paths. However, the recent upsurge in this activity is such that mountain bikers are asked to safeguard their future by acting in a considerate manner when on hill

The art of the drystane dyker is one of the many fascinations for an appreciative eye in the heart of the hills.

paths. It is suggested that bikers should:
1. Give way to pedestrians
2. Keep strictly to public paths
3. Avoid paths on steep peat ground
4. Refrain from 'locking up' the rear wheel
5. 'Carry' over deep soft muddy areas'

You might as well ask the rain to fall only during the night. The most cursory observation of the Pentlands will show that mountain biking cheerfully ignores all of these 'suggestions' and will go on doing so as long as 'mountain biking is recognised as a legitimate use of public paths'. Recognised by whom, incidentally? Given that the park has issued its code, does it then crank the bureaucratic machine into action by monitoring response to its 'suggestions'? If it does, is it not missing the point, namely that once it starts making authoritarian statements, however 'suggestive', it then starts to respond to its own authority in the role of policeman. It is the worst kind of fate for a ranger service, but it is happening, and it is happening in the Pentland Hills. It is as much of an intrusion as the mountain biker, and Will Grant must be birling furiously in his grave.

I stood within a yard or two of the Cauldstane Slap path while six bikers whooped past. The predominant colours were pink, orange, lime green, turquoise and yellow. Not only did they not give way to the only pedestrian in sight, they did not even acknowledge my presence. I acknowledged theirs alright, with a crude gesture at their retreating backs which did not dignify the case for the opposition. But such encounters cause real anger and resentment. It is not the future of the mountain bikers which should be safeguarded, but the future of the hills.

I cannot believe that a mild cautionary note and a haphazard policing of its recommendations by rangers is either an effective or an appropriate deterrent, yet I know from my own experiences and from many and widespread outbursts at bikers in wild places that an effective deterrent needs to be found – not to satisfy the self-centred interests of the solitary wanderer who craves the peace of the hills, but to satisfy the interests of the peace of the hills itself. It is the landscape itself which should be the first consideration of all of us who trek the Pentlands, whatever our motives. I can see no other solution to the particular dilemma of mountain bikers in wild places other than making them feel unwelcome. Passive and pointed resistance by walkers and estates might do the trick.

I seethed most of the way up East Cairn Hill, and finally channeled my anger into one specific logical protest. It is that the majority of hill folk in a place like the Pentlands comprise a loose, unwritten and fraternal fellowship. The fellowship is a thing of the hills themselves, and the bikers breach that fellowship, and it is as simple as that.

I reached the summit of East Cairn Hill much mollified by the dyke which graces its eastern shoulder and plunges far into the northern hills. It is a subtle and substantial masterpiece among dykes and I never fail to marvel at it. But I had been on the summit for no more than five minutes when I was forcibly wrenched back into that mountain bike controversy.

A girl appeared over the edge of the hill's summit plateau, having climbed from the head of the Slap, and now paused to scan the pass through binoculars. As she paused, she leaned for a respite on her travelling companion – a mountain bike. She pushed it to the summit, where she offered a monosyllabic greeting, then disappeared along the summit ridge of the hill. Her jacket bore the unmistakeable badge of the countryside ranger.

How did it go again '… legitimate use of public paths … keep strictly to the public paths … avoid steep peat ground …'. Every aspect of the regional park's work convinces me that it is the province of the wrong kind of people in the wrong place for the wrong reasons. A handful of honourable exceptions do not mitigate this overwhelming bludgeon effect of the majority.

I walked back to the sanity of the dyke. The sun and the

wind had lit up the landscape again, and now struck rich seams of colour and glinting light. The darkest greys glowed purple, the palest faded to blue, and silver darted everywhere the light struck a tiny ridge or flaky edge. The style of the dyke's construction intrigued. The lowest third of it was built with stones laid more or less horizontally. Above that, a single row of protruding stones ran the entire length of the dyke, almost like an embellishment for the sake of ornament, although they also fulfil the practical purpose of a step ladder for climbing the dyke. The top half of the dyke, however, was what stamped a definitive character on its craftsmanship, for it was made entirely of long, flat and narrow stones, laid on end, so that the entire thrust of the dyke suddenly became vertical.

It gives an effect of delicacy to the whole structure, yet, its secret is its strength, the tall stones so tightly wedged, one against the other, that I found no moveable stone in fifty yards of dyke – at seven or eight stones a yard, call it four hundred stones.

These dykes embody all that today's attitudes to the hills do not – patience, art, and a long-term sense of values appropriate to the nature of the landscape. The materials are of the landscape, and the art of the dyker is coloured and shaped by the colour and shape of the landscape. When the dyke eventually collapses, it can be rebuilt with the same stones which have fallen out of place. Too often, though, they are replaced where they rot by fences (increasingly by electric fences), and when fences collapse they are replaced by new fences, and usually the old ones are left to rot and rust alongside. Where is the art in an electric fence? Where is the acknowledgement of landscape? A new fence I encountered on Byrehope Mount, far across the Slap, was punctuated by plastic tags which fluttered and flashed in the wind – advertisements for the fence manufacturer which also bore the legend 'Made in England'. Give me a dyke, signed by the hand of its own dyker, and made in Scotland right where it stands.

The park, the bikes, the fences are just symbols, symptomatic of a philosophy and a way of life which distance people from the hills. For all that Edinburgh now laps the feet of Allermuir and Caerketton, it has never been further removed psychologically from the hills than it is now. Yet even here, in the heartland hills of the Pentlands, Edinburgh has tainted the wildness of the place with the scent of the urban thinking behind the regional park.

Surely, this deep into the hills, any authority which claimed to have the welfare of the hills at heart would champion the simplistic philosophy of a pair of good boots, the joy of discovery, the worth of wild landscape, the art of a mile of built stone, and it would ensure in the process that its own hand was quite invisible. But they don't make parks that way, and the sight of a ranger, with or without a mountain bike, on the hills of the Cauldstane Slap is a dismaying trend.

The long moorland trek up to the Cauldstane Slap is one way into the heartland hills. The Kirk Road and the higher moor track over the Kitchen Moss are others, utterly different in character, but just as redolent of the essence of the Pentland Hills. A third and quite unique variation on the theme is the right-of-way from Buteland to Carlops, where a mile-long avenue of hawthorn trees escorts you over the high fields and moors which lie between the Lanark Road and the country of the Boar Stane. The right-of-way is another of those trans-Pentland crossings and the most furtive of them all for the way it slips between folds in the hills.

But first you must reach the hills, and before that – why Buteland? It is the unlikeliest of destinations or beginnings for a right-of-way, for it's only a farm, and neither on the Old Lanark Road (a fragment of which skirts the Scottish Wildlife Trust reserve at Red Moss) nor the new. It is there the route begins, anyway, with its dead-straight mile of hawthorns, on both sides of the road. The avenue has been thickened over the years by a shelter belt of conifers, so that visual impact

One of the Pentlands' most delightful old green roads burrows into the hills from the Boar Stane, making for the North Esk Reservoir.

is played down (the conifers have long since dwarfed the hawthorns). But at any season, especially its late spring blossoming, the hawthorns have a way of stamping their character on your walk. The sight and scent of the blossoming is its finest hour, inevitably, and like walking through a dense growth of bog-myrtle, the scent seems to cling to you and insinuate the air long after you have left its source behind. The berry season puts a new shade on the avenue, a vivid scarlet deluge, and as with the blossom, the regular placements of the trees at intervals of a few yards along a mile-long straight turns a common feat of nature into a spectacular. Finches and tits and warblers use the trees as thoroughfares, but as autumn deepens, the berry-pirates arrive, looting and pillaging down the land from Scandinavia, the redwings and fieldfares. Their boisterous flocks, augmented by sporadic gatherings of waxwings, turn any thicket of hawthorn into a small orgy. Somehow this formalised avenue has the effect of curbing their brasher excesses, but the place is well known to the thrush tribes, and whatever decorum the layout demands, there are

The Boar Stane is a contemplative kind of place with a subtle atmosphere, a sense of presence, a folded away place. The origin of its name is, at best, a piece of guesswork.

berries enough to last a lot of birds for a long time.

The metalled road ends abruptly, and with it the trees. It is as if a curtain has suddenly been peeled aside, for you are suddenly confronted with as wide a sweep of the Pentlands as you see from any close vantage point, as far up as the 'back' of Allermuir, as far down as West Cairn Hill. The Kips and Scald Law stand aloof beyond the rise of Hare Hill and the dour preponderance of Black Hill. It is a startling transition both in landscape terms and in the traveller's frame of mind, for the hawthorn avenue has an introverting effect on a train of thought; the sudden panorama derails it.

Rough grazing, moorland, fine old pine remnants, a kestrel working the moor, an old railway wagon doubling as a feed store for beasts and rusting in a curiously captivating way, a heather-scented breeze mingling with the aftermath of hawthorn, the skyline scatter of the Boar Stane's tree sentinels ... these are the characteristics of the new world. The stile which conducts you from metalled road to hill

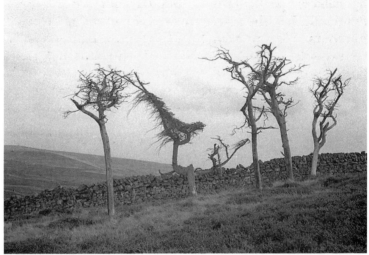

A gaunt gathering of dead trees stands near the Boar Stane, tortured by all manner of high winds, an eerie assembly on a misty day.

track confronts you with one more example of the dykes-versus-fences controversy. There is a new fence. There is an old and ruinous dyke. And there is a quite beautifully fashioned stone gatepost standing alone, unattached to dyke or gate, its purpose supplanted by a new timber gate. I patted its curving crown, a consoling gesture for both of us.

So I mounted the hill track with the grouse 'go-back'-ing at me and a deep, rich blueness in the pines, a warm wind out of the south, and the kind of light which throws a haze over every horizon but sharpens the near hills to needlepoints. It is a fine approach to the hills, and the track threads and curves up through the contours in a particularly inviting way. The higher it climbs, however, the more it deteriorates, the result of the regular passage over fragile ground of Land-Rovers and other hill-going vehicles. Railway sleepers have been laid down over the worst of it, and the result is a very unflattering mess.

Something needs to be put into perspective here. We constantly hear about the damage caused to the countryside by walkers, particularly in popular hill areas like the Pentlands; it is the result, we are told, of an explosion of numbers. We are usually told this by landowners or countryside bureaucrats, which often amounts to the same thing. Indeed, the popularity of the Pentlands is one of the reasons offered for setting up the Pentland Hills Regional Park. What is not being said is that the worst abuses of the Pentlands landscape – and the landscapes of other popular mountain areas like the Cairngorms and Glencoe – are often caused by landowners, not walkers.

No amount of walking causes the kind of damage which has been inflicted on Black Hill, or the defiling of Castlelaw by the Army, or the dereliction of woodlands all over the Pentlands, or the degrading of the land by overgrazing.

Clearly there are good landowners and bad, and there are walkers who make us all wince with embarrassment, but the strident nature of many landowners' protests at walkers and conservationists, and their bellicose pronouncements about access, are substantial distortions of the reality on the ground.

There is no erosion by hordes of feet on the Boar Stane path, but there is landowner-inflicted erosion, and enough of a glimpse of the Black Hill wound to bear in mind that this is no isolated lapse.

The track climbs to another handsome dyke at the head of the pass, beyond which it dips and swerves gently down into the deepest recesses of the hill, accompanied by the companionable march of a second dyke, and briefly, by the Henshaw Burn. There are no more hill-swaddled places in the Pentlands than Henshaw Burn where it lopes down under Deerhope Rig and Cock Rig for the North Esk Reservoir. As you stand at the summit of the pass, the western hills swoop down in long diagonals – Deerhope Rig, Wether Law, The Mount, Fairliehope Hill – while the path seems to burrow down under the steeper slopes of Cock Rig and Spittal Hill. It is a softer landscape than Cauldstane Slap or Kitchen Moss, but it is just as quintessentially Pentlands.

Of all the prospects into the hills from their own passes, this is the one which most cheerfully wins me over.

Part of the charm of that pass stems from an outcrop of rock and a rag-and-tatters band of aged larches, some of them dead but still standing in skeletal accusations. And in the nearest end of the trees is another flat rock for all the world like nature's answer to a garden bench. Many a contemplative fag has been smoked here. You can tell that because many a contemplative fag-end has been stubbed out on the turf.

It is a contemplative kind of place, though, for the outcrop with it's kite's tail of trees straggling uphill is called the Boar Stane. Or the Bore Stane. Or the Bore Stone. I go for Boar Stane, because in a Pentlands context I find 'stone' unthinkable; and because if we have got the sound of the first word right it's much more likely to have been a stane where a wild boar lived or at least fed and foraged than a borestone where the standard of an unknown battle flew. The problem with scratching the surface of a small dilemma like this is that it doesn't answer even the small questions, and tends to replace the small questions with big ones. Of the obvious sources of reference, all four variations of spelling are used, although Boar Stane edges out the others. The most recent, on the regional park's map, Bore Stane, appears, but as this is the map which missed out the wood at the Martyr's Tomb and called Gap Law 'Cap Law', and advises walkers to stick to public footpaths only, you should take a fairly relaxed attitude towards it.

The Boar Stane, then, is a place of subtle atmosphere, a sense of presence – not a presence in the sense of the supernatural or lurking wild boar, but of a folded-away place. Although it is just a few yards from the head of the pass, and although the rocks themselves are part of a brave little heathery mound, the place is actually in a hollow. The sound of the hill wind – an ever-present song on an exposed hillside wide open to the west – is changed by the presence of the trees, to something both softer and more brittle, more uneven and disturbed.

The trees look as if they have been rinsed clean and blow dried – rain, wind, rain, wind, and fitful sun – into a perpetual but vigorous dishevelment. The dead ones recall the famous quip by Sidney Smith, often a hillgoing companion of Lord Cockburn at Bonaly, but who found his Lordship's pace a bit much. On a hot day he wisecracked: 'I wish I could put off my flesh and sit in my bones and let the wind whistle through them.' If you wonder how such a feat might have turned out, there is a tree at the Boar Stane which offers a possible likeness.

The rocks of the Boar Stane are slabby and pink, and when you sit among them you can feel as secure as their fissure-rooted heather and lichens. Somehow they pull you into their own hill rootedness and because they are in a hollow and not thrust out on a crag or a high moor, it is a pull which you feel inclined to submit to and immerse yourself in its aura. It is a good place, the Boar Stane, but hard as I have tried, I'm damned if I can imagine the place overrun with wild boar. Wild boar were woodland animals, and although the Pentlands' western slopes were undoubtedly thicker-wooded when boar were around – up to the seventeenth century – the Boar Stane is at 1300 feet, and the nearby larches show how well trees fare here. Perhaps there was a famous hunt which had its dénouement here. Perhaps there was a famous carved stone (wild boar are among the very oldest of carved rock symbols in Scotland) which went the way of the Monks Road cross. Perhaps we've been handed down the wrong word altogether. Perhaps it would be Bear Stane ... But it is a good place to while away a Pentland hour.

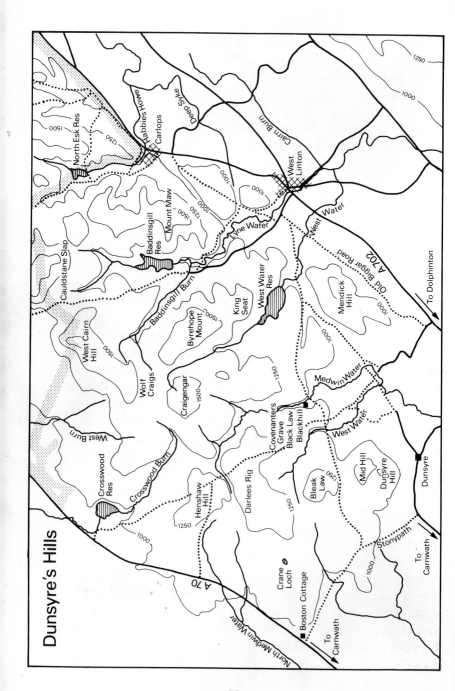

Dunsyre's Hills

To Dolphinton

1250

1000

Cairn Burn

West Linton

West Water

Old Biggar Road

A702

Mendick Hill

1000

1000

Rabbies Howe

Carlops

Deep Syke

North Esk Res

1500

1250

1000

Cauldstane Slap

Baddinsgill Res

Mount Maw

1500

1250

1000

Lyne Water

West Water Res

King Seat

Byrehope Mount

1500

Baddinsgill Burn

West Cairn Hill

1500

Wolf Craigs

Craigengar

1500

1250

Medwin Water

Covenanters Grave

Black Law

Blackhill

1250

West Water

Mid Hill

Bleak Law

Dunsyre Hill

Dunsyre

To Carnwath

Stonypath

Darlees Rig

Henshaw Hill

1250

Crosswood Res

Crosswood Burn

West Burn

1000

A70

1250

Crane Loch

Boston Cottage

To Carnwath

1000

North Medwin Water

To Carnwath

CHAPTER 4

Dunsyre's Hills

The hills west and south of the Cauldstane Slap end at
Dunsyre. Some will tell you that the Pentlands begin at
Dunsyre and end at the Slap, and now that the regional park
lurks up-by, they wouldn't be seen dead east of the Slap. Oh,
this is more than a one-man vendetta against the park, you
know! Scratch most Pentland plodders of any vintage and
you'll unleash an unstaunchable blood-letting diatribe
against the whole ill-advised motley of park people. They
didn't want it, didn't ask for it, and don't see a shred of
evidence to justify it. So they either ignore it, or a few of
them, commendable purists to the core, stay west of the
Slap.

They inhabit the land furtively, like a wounded Covenanter
fleeing from Rullion Green. They tend to be solitary chiels,
not given to walking in parties, fond of the hills' solaces and
silences, but cheerful enough when you encounter them,
because the chances are, you'll be there for much the same
reason. The hills match their needs, a lower-profile tribe,
subtler, wide open on the surface but saving their best for
the intimacies of cleuch and syke. They speak with a thicker
tongue too – Black Birn, Yield Brae, Lingy Knowe, Bawdy
Moss, Bassy Burn, Fingerstane Cleuch ....The small
intimacies of such places can shake your head in wonder.
The dome-ish summit plateau of the high ground, like
Byrehope Mount or Craigengar, is the roof of all that world,
a heady elevation such as you do not experience on the
higher, sharper-defined summits of the north Pentlands.
There are fewer tracks and long heathery miles down here,
a landscape painted in broader brushstrokes, and with a
restrained hand. Yet that same understated impression can
be misleading, for you can emerge from a fifteen-mile
round trek in these southern Pentland Hills sorely tried by

The Wolf Craigs ... 'one of the few places in the Pentlands where you can feel utterly shut in and isolated'. Fugitive Covenanters knew it well.

the terrain and the wind, and if you choose winter, by the snow's passion in such landscapes for smoothing over the ditches and sykes and holes ... all the things you are likely to fall into when soft snow catches you unawares.

Dunsyre's hills begin for me with the Wolf Craigs, and end with Dunsyre. There is a reason for this although it's one which probably only makes sense to me, and the one I call The Artist. It is that I first encountered the Wolf Craigs in the company of The Artist, and we came in by a circuitous route of his own devising from Dunsyre, threading all his Pentlands preferences and prejudices together in a single journey. There is more to it than that, though, and perhaps the reasoning will rub off as this exploration of these hills unfolds. At the Wolf Craigs, The Artist proclaimed that this was the northern limit of his territory and he could no more cross the Slap now than he could take up mountain biking. He had dismissed all beyond the Slap as a write-off, bedevilled by the park and its walk-this-way mentality which is as demeaning to walkers as it is to the Pentland Hills.

So he prowled the hills between here and Dunsyre Hill, between Mendick and Henshaw, Torweaving and Kingseat, and a jaunt up West Cairn Hill was flirting with the devil. It's not that The Artist doesn't know the hills beyond the Slap, for he was an Edinburgh South-sider, but he's given up on them. He's not the first, and not the last either, but for one who feels the Call of the Pentlands so profoundly, it is a tragedy that he felt obliged to choose. The regional park manufacturers will rubbish all that as sentimental nonsense, of course, but rubbishing true hill instincts is one of the few things they do well.

So down here is The Artist's soul country, and Black Law with its Covenanter's Grave is his Dunadd. As I write this, he is 'no jist as bauld as aince I wess', as MacDiarmid has it, the result of a malfunction of the kist, and for the time being at least, has had to take it easier on the tramping, but still I can't sit under the pock-marked overhangs of the Wolf Craigs without something of the man accompanying me there. That is not to suggest that the Artist is anyway pock-marked and overhanging, only that an ounce or two of the soul of the man is almost visible, clinging to the rocks like a brooding kestrel. The Pentlands have coursed through all his lives – Edinburgh youth, National Service soldier, shipwright, internationally acclaimed muralist, mosaicist and stained-glass artist, and now journalist, poet and author. His art was both blessed and hamstrung by the fact that he had built ships, his journalism by the eloquence of his art, his poetry by the working-class rootedness of his journalism.

The man is to be found in his element either quaffing lumps of salt air in the Orkney of his forebears (the words 'I'm a Garson' are a passport which opens many doors in those islands) or here under the Wolf Craigs. The salt of the earth does not come much purer than The Artist, and I never once regretted an hour of his company. So when I gang my ain gait amid the flocked solitudes of these southern Pentlands, I pause an hour under the Wolf Craigs and find company of a kind there.

An old ruined cottage deep in the hills above the Baddinsgill Burn, a formidably lonely place, now the haunt of kestrels and mice, owls and foxes.

It may be difficult to conjure up wild boar at the Boar Stane, but the Wolf Craigs is an eminently wolfish place. It is one of the few places in the Pentlands where you can feel utterly shut in and isolated, and you rarely share it in any season with other signs of life, save the wind-working kestrels and the summer cloudberries.

It is no surprise to learn that the Covenanters felt secure in the small chasm between the two main rock outcrops (or at least as secure as they ever felt, for when they were out of sight in the hills, so were their pursuers). One of the outcrops is a heather-backed knoll hacked into immense boulders, the other a low and fractured crag, deeply indented and overhung, and set into the top of a steep heathery bank. Between the two, a sliver of the Baddinsgill Burn's headwaters sometimes flows, or sometimes – at the end of a drearily dry summer, for example – it doesn't bother.

It wasn't bothering on an October day of charitable Indian summer warmth, when I slipped into the south end of the Slap and side-tracked round Muckle Knock to that plaintive old bothy ruin above the Baddinsgill Burn. The writers of bad Scottish songs always used to have lines like:

Awa' in the Hielans there stands a wee hoose,
It stands on the breist o' the brae…

I think they never went to the Hielans. I think they inhabited Edinburgh garrets and strolled up the Baddinsgill Burn to that point where the burn skips down a rocky leap or two, and its banks frame the breist of Muckle Knock's brae and its wee hoose, and their dewy imaginations did the rest. And how many of them could have withstood a day and night alone in such a place? Even now, with the old quarry track running yards from what's left of the door, with the benevolent autumn sun striking sparks in the lintel, and with a shepherd's voice bellowing to his dogs above the engine noise of his four-wheel-drive shepherd's buggy high up on Whauplie Rig, it is still a formidably lonely looking cottage. I people it with lives as I pass – a hird, a hermit, an old crone some folk called 'witch', a summer lover and his lass, a lost hill gangrel, a mouse, a swallow, an owl, a fox. A kestrel stands on an unseen pedestal above the chimney and steps off on wing points, sliding off on the wind. I salute all the lives of the cottage's life and death, and slide away over the hill myself, following the burn.

The burn forks. The Wolf Craigs huddle up at the top end of the south fork. If you were to come on them from above, they look like nothing at all, a gray pause in the flow of the moor – nothing much. But they grow impressive as you near them until when you stand under them you feel almost as if the hills have laid a trap for you and snapped it shut.

For all that you now stand under Craigengar and Byrehope Mount, you see nothing of them, at least nothing that hints at their expansive heights. The Wolf Craigs demand introspection, and the study of landscape on a small scale. There is a certain recess where the wind – all winds, it seems – are beaten back and the sun floods in. I put my back to the

The Covenanter's Grave on Black Hill marks the last resting place of a fugitive from the Battle of Rullion Green, and commemorates one of the Pentlands' most extraordinary stories.

old rock where perhaps a wolf bitch once lay with one eye on the summer's cantering cubs, the other on a bleeding, limping man dragging a useless leg across the hills, hugging the low ground, avoiding the skyline, looking fearfully over his shoulder. The wolf would see him struggle over a shoulder of Craigengar, where he could slip down into Ravens Cleuch and follow the Medwin Water down to the remote cottage of Blackhill. He was John Carphin, an Ayrshire man, one of the band that had tormented Turner in the south-west and marched on Edinburgh brandishing their faith before them and singing psalms, until Dalyell settled their hash at Rullion Green. The Covenanter was dying from his wounds when he blundered in on Adam Sanderson, hird, who lived at Blackhill. Sanderson tried to press hospitality and care on him, but the Covenanter was driven by two fears. One was that in the aftermath of Rullion Green there would be trouble for all those who harboured fugitives, and he had no wish to inflict that on such a kindly man of the hills. The second was that he might die where he was not in sight of the Ayrshire hills.

Sanderson refused to abandon Carphin and went with him up the West Water, but at a spot Sanderson knew as Oaken Bush, Carphin's wounds got the better of his courage and he died. Sanderson honoured the man's last wish and buried him on Black Law where a gap in the hills spears through to the hills of the south-west. A stone, roughly carved in a code which would baffle the dragoons if they found it, marked the spot, but has long since been moved to Dunsyre Kirk. The present stone at what the maps now mark as The Covenanter's Grave is much later. Reith gives this account of the sequel of that day in 1666, citing an article in the *Weekly Scotsman* of 1907 which in turn cited *Blackwood's Magazine* of October 1817.

'An enterprising youth, a farmer's son in the Easdon district [a farm near Dunsyre], went to the top of the hill with a spade with a view to discovering whether tradition was correct in declaring that this spot was the Covenanter's grave. He began to dig, and speedily found what he was after. He came home in triumph with a skull, some pieces of cloth, and a few brass buttons, but his father, a true-blue Presbyterian, indignant at the desecration of a spot hallowed to the mind of every patriotic Scotsman, first administered a severe thrashing to his son, and then went with him to re-inter the sacred relics ... It was then resolved to mark the spot with a permanent monument ....'

A note, quoting the *Weekly Scotsman,* adds: '... it was at the instigation of Dr. Manuel, minister of Dunsyre, and mainly at his expense, that the tombstone was set up about the year 1841.'

Why this should spill out and preoccupy me up-by at the Wolf Craigs – apart from obvious Covenanting associations – has to do with my friend The Artist, alias George Garson. The alias has to drop now because it is George Garson, poet, rather than Artist, who set down this episode in the Pentlands' story more tellingly than any other. His poem begins with

the words and the shape of an inscription on that stone of
1841 which still stands on a shoulder of Black Law:

SACRED

To the memory of

A COVENANTER

who fought and was wounded

at Rullion Green

Nov 28th 1666

and who died at Oaken Bush

the day after the Battle

and was buried here

BY ADAM SANDERSON

OF BLACKHILL

BEFORE THE BATTLE

Come first light, his commonplace skyline
ran mad with curses and pikes.

He had slept fitfully on his strae bed,
listening…
The nocturnal raspings of stoat and rat
riven by alien tongues and the yelp of steel.

A gaunt straggle:
some had guns with rusty ratches;
others the coulter of a plough,
scythes and spades.
Some had halbards, forks and flails.

'The Almichty bless the shieling, hird.
Nae ill tae ye guidman.
Oor fecht lies furth o' your bit dykes and fanks.
But pray for us.
For Protestant bluid micht weel smitch
your puckle knowes gin dayset.'

Weaned on the moor's elemental creed,
he mumbled rough blessing on the day
and called his dog to heel;
flummoxed by the grim tenets of kirk and Covenant.

Inching into sleep that night,
he pondered on the Westland man:
a shilpit chiel.
Yellow hair slaggered to his brow
by winter's ceaseless blash.
Legs clad in hoggers of straw
bound with rags
Unaware that, come dawn,
he'd spade down the bairn's sword-bitten corpse
in a shallow hillside grave.

Sanderson's house is ruinous now. A blaze of rowan berries is all the fire that warms the place. You come upon its weary isolation if you wander up the Medwin Water from Medwynbank – and no, nobody seems to have the slightest idea why they spell themselves differently – or trek the drove road in from Boston Cottage on the Lanark Road. The river there, by way of confusing the hill gangrel, is the North Medwin Water, despite the fact that it's due west of the Medwin Water, but folk have been confusing compass points in the Pentlands for as long as they have been giving them names.

Elsewhere around this end of the hills you will find two West Waters, both of which flow south-east, and about three miles apart. Needless to say, there is no East Water. There is a Left Law followed by a Mid Hill, and no Right Law; there is a North Muir Hill but you search in vain for a south one.

Sanderson's walls are less than waist-high in places now, but here and there, too, they have been thoughtfully and recently patched with the ruin's own fallen stone. It is the work of The Artist, going in about the place on his many stravaigings through the south Pentlands, paying his small

The remains of Adam Sanderson's cottage at Blackhill on the Medwin Water. It was Sanderson who comforted the wounded Covenanter after Rullion Green, then buried him in sight of his native Ayrshire hills.

homage to the good man of Blackhill. His years of creating mosaics with natural materials, notably slate, have given him an easy familiarity with the art of laying stone on stone so that it 'reads'. It is an artist's eye – or a poet's – that he turns on the Pentlands' repertoire of drystane dykes, but he knows the trick of fashioning the strength at the heart of them too. He's built ships, you see.

So that's what slips in and out of my mind's eye in an hour hunkered down by the Wolf Craigs over the hill. Sanderson might well have been familiar with the passing tread of wolf, although by the mid-1600s, they were dwindling down the path to extinction, especially in these south lands. Surer by far, was that he would know otters in the burn at his door. He would know herons too, for they still make a fearful tumult in the early spring branches of the pinewood up the Medwin Water, and their cries are everywhere on the water, even though the otters have gone, bar the odd passing stranger fussing through the banks and the bracken and the burns in search of Tweed, perhaps. But Sanderson would know encounters like this:

'And so it was that Old Nog, the wisest heron of the Two Rivers, heard the noise of bubbles breaking on the water as he alighted by the pool side. He watched, prepared to jump-and-flap if there was danger. He saw a swirl of water, and the roll of two dark sleek bodies. He waited. They rolled nearer. With neck and beak held low – a two-pointed horn spear on a shaft hidden by long narrow feathers – he waded into water over his knee joints. While he paused for a plunge of the spear, which had pierced and held many a rat and eel, the bitch's head arose a yard from him, and at her sharp cry the cubs fell apart and swam under. The heron, with a harsh squawk of anger and alarm, jumped into the air and beat slowly away, the legs stretched out behind him, and neck tucked between his lean shoulders. *Krack* cried Old Nog, as he flew to his next fishing place.'

Thus the great Henry Williamson described a fleeting encounter between Tarka and Old Nog, and Sanderson would have nodded his agreement at the perfection of detail which ensnares the encounter. If there was ever to be a badge of the Pentlands, in the way that Shetland brandishes puffins and red-throated divers and Speyside its ospreys, it should feature Old Nog lifting from a burn with a stand of pines at his back and the curve of Black Law for a skyline.

I hope such a badge is never made, but there is something in the sight and sound and stealth of herons going about their everyday lives which smacks of the marrow of the Pentland Hills. It is a thing in its place, and it is as simple as that.

The Artist and I were padding up the Medwin, rounding the pinewood, dropping through the bracken to the burnside when the local Old Nog neck-straightened in his favourite pool, head-wheeled, spread a wide blanket of wings, raised the undercarriage of his legs. As he climbed from the burn, his shadow fell across the walls of Sanderson's cottage, and the sight of it stopped me dead. How many shadows of how many herons have done that throughout the life and death of the cottage – say four hundred years?

When there was a roof to the walls, old Sanderson would see the shadow of the birds slide down it to the pool. He would see the otter's bubble-wake foraging upstream, and see the shadow climb the house again as the bird leapt in slow alarm. Sometimes the shadow would have a writhing eel on the 'two-pointed horn spear' as the bird was disturbed while wrestling with its catch. In that way, or some other, thousands of heron shadows have darkened Sanderson's window, and scaled his walls.

The particular Old Nog that The Artist and I disturbed unleashed a dipper from a mid-burn rock. The art of flight has few greater extremes than these two – the slow unfurling of heron sails and the blunt, headlong blur of the burn-clinging dipper. Yet when the dipper goes underwatering to feed on the river bed, he too becomes a wing-unfurler, his wingbeats slow as a heron, and we flight-watchers on the bank fell into a fascinating and quite futile debate about the wiles and mysteries of bird flight.

The 'kraak' in the sky lifted our dipper-hypnotised eyes to the edge of the wood where two more herons and then one more rounded the bend in the burn, homing in on the pool. But then there was us, coffee-supping and cracking open the hard-boiled eggs, and the herons, being sharp-eyed as well as sharp-nebbed and sharp-kneed, dispersed on the wind with the thistledown.

One turned and sailed in over the wood, stalled on fabulous wing-flexing brakes and perched halfway up an old pine. The only thing which looks more ridiculous up a tree than a heron is a cormorant, but then that's a judgement of non-tree-perching humans and based more on aesthetics than hard-headed scientific assessment. Herons, of course, are born to it, and although a big spring wind can take a fearful toll on a heronry by blowing the young from the treetop nests, the survivors learn that even if there is no food for a heron up a tree, there can be shelter, and more important, safety for a bird which is notoriously slow off the mark.

This one was a Young Nog, a new generation on the Medwin Water, but when he settled his neck back into his shoulders and put his wings out in the hill air, his shadow fell down the bracken bank, across the burn, up the far back and rippled over the walls and the hearth and the ash tree of Blackhill. As long as there are Old Nogs and Young flying under the Pentlands sun, and a thoughtful hand to ply a dyker's labour of love on Sanderson's old place, things will stay that way.

'Here they disturbed Old Nog,' wrote Williamson, 'who was overlooking one of his many fishing places along the valley. *Krark!* He flapped away before them, his long, thin, green toes scratching the water.'

The land you tramp when you go in search of Covenanter relics and Old Nogs is part of the 2000-acre estate of Colonel Sutherland of Ferniehaugh whose family have owned the land since the 1920s. Robbie Steven, shepherd in particular and estate manager in general, has the same relationship with the Colonel that his father had with the Colonel's father. That kind of continuity is rare today in the Scottish landscape, and where you still find it, you tend to find a degree of enlightenment in the management of the land born of loyalty – loyalty to the people on the estate (and at Ferniehaugh that is conspicuously two-way) and loyalty to the land.

Yet Colonel Sutherland lives and works in London. He is, by his own admission, one of that most untrusted of species in the Scottish landscape, an absentee landlord, and runs his estate 'by remote control'. When I went to see him to discuss his land and attitude towards it, it was he who raised the subject, and defended it thus: 'A lot of people see absentee landowners as bad news, but these things always have two sides to them. If I didn't live and work in London much of the time, I wouldn't have the cash to run this place as I do.'

It is when you see the way he does run it that that
questionable precept becomes a sustainable argument.
The first thing you notice as you approach Ferniehaugh is
the trees, in their variety, and of every age. Many are newly
planted, many in vigorous youth, many in their lofty prime
– and they are trees not planted for their value as a cash-crop
harvest, but for their intrinsic value as trees, trees for their
own sake. It is a symptom of the simple philosophy at the
core of Colonel Sutherland's management of the land:
'You must look after the elements.'

Elements? 'The heather, the wildlife, the trees, the water,
the skyline, the dykes. I'm always trying to improve the
property, not just for myself and my family, but for everyone
else as well.'

Much of his energy on that score has gone into tree
planting and thinning and improving the quality and the
spread of heather. The trees, particularly, are a labour of
love, and given that the estate lies almost wholly between
900ft and 1500ft above sea level and on one of the windier
tracts of upland Scotland, it is not a simple passion to
indulge. As the Colonel put it: 'Timber here grows in
corkscrews.' But with the skills of a firm of timber consultants,
a programme of plantation thinning (the modest profit
from that going into new planting, hardwoods for conifers,
a straight and enlightened swop), and his own love of
planting beautiful trees for the sake of having beautiful
trees, it is an increasingly healthy and attractive environment
which evolves at Ferniehaugh.

'I don't say that it would be unliveable here without the
woods, but it would be very much less attractive. The
benefits are not just for wildlife and shelter for stock.
They're also visual.'

Improving the heather is the Colonel's other *cause célèbre*.
It is all too rare to hear a Scottish landowner bemoan the
effects of overgrazing by sheep, but Colonel Sutherland
concedes that here, and in many other place in the Pentlands,
the hills have suffered from overgrazing. He has already

begun to remedy the situation, putting off sheep and using the latest techniques for removing the hill grasses which inhibit heather, and generally creating a better hill climate for heather to flourish.

'No heather, no grouse,' he explained, 'and no grouse is bad news.'

The grouse are becoming an increasingly important economic factor as sheep become less important, but just as the trees serve several purposes, not the least of them aesthetic, so does the heather. What is good for the grouse is also good for the other heather-loving birds – merlins, short-eared owls, hen harriers, for example – and these sleeker, rounder Pentlands are at their best under a dense cover of healthy heather.

Colonel Sutherland regrets the passing of the days when many a Pentlands shepherd would be up at dawn every day to lift sheep from their overnight hillside and drive them to a different part of the hill to spend the day feeding. Then he would drive them back in the evening, literally, to their sleeping quarters, thus controlling grazing patterns on the hill.

Now, though, the long dominance of sheep may be on the wane, a return to the days, in these hills at least, of forty or fifty years ago when 'there were far fewer sheep and many more grouse'.

Many more people too. The environment of Ferniehaugh is enriched by ponds, and high in the hills, by an old man-made Victorian pleasure garden, long overgrown: and this too is being painstakingly restored, part of the Colonel's avowed aim of 'improving the property and passing it on to my son in good nick'.

The biggest single threat to the wellbeing of these southern Pentland Hills, and one which he is 'terrified of', is the ever-present prospect of *ad hoc* development, of roads being run into the hills for housing and tourist developments like caravan sites. 'Caravan sites,' he said, using his all-purpose expression of profound disapproval, 'are bad news.' He

speaks on the subject with some feeling, as one who went to
the trouble and expense of building even his sheep sheds
well out of sight.

Colonel Sutherland's lifelong association with these hills
is at the heart of his philosophy. Such an attachment to a
piece of ground makes 'an enormous difference'. It also
means a keen sensitivity to changes on the ground. At
Ferniehaugh, that means fewer grouse, partridge and the
demise of black grouse. Small birds, however, have increased
dramatically, the result of all the new trees. A big influx of
geese is the biggest single visible change, and grey squirrels
have taken over from red. Dykers, farriers, wheelwrights
and a dozen other species of rural craftsmen have all but
faded away, although he is convinced that the dyking art is
on its way back, assisted by fifty per cent grants and
encouraging noises from the Department of Agriculture.

An intriguing aside, and one which confounds the
bureaucratic empire of the northern Pentlands, is that
there are fewer people walking the hills and paths of the
southern Pentlands than there were thirty or forty years
ago. As it is a central plank of regional park philosophy that
their regime is necessary because of greatly increased
numbers on the hills, perhaps it is time to consider whether
or not this perceived problem of too many walkers is
exacerbated by the existence of the park itself. Provide the
facilities, particularly car parks, publicise them, and stand
back while the effect of such a policy destroys that which is
supposed to be being protected.

An hour in Colonel Sutherland's company goes a long
way to restoring faith in the healthy future of the Pentland
Hills through enlightened management. I asked him how
he would like to see the hills managed in the future. He said:
'Encourage those who want to improve the environment.
Look after the heather, trees, water, dykes. Get back to the
natural heather-clad hills we used to have.'

Earlier in our conversation he had waved a hand at Black
Hill which dominates a side window of his study at

Ferniehaugh, and said: 'I'm very keen on the hills themselves, the changing light and seasons, and the skyline. They are well rounded hills, and they give a certain amount of contentment.' I left him feeling a certain amount of contentment about the future at least of these southern Pentland Hills, that he will see to it that they are handed on 'in good nick', which is all any of us can ask of those who hold our cherished landscape in their care. May his wise influence rub off on others.

The south-west hills of the Pentlands are among the least trampled of all southern Scotland's hills, an unimaginable Pentland landscape when you first survey the world of Edinburgh and the Forth from Caerketton. You have left the park and the Lothians behind here, and the hills masquerade as Strathclyde if you please. It's not such an idiotic arrangement as some corners of that bizarre monolith – like Mull, say, or Glen Orchy – for the waters of these lowly Pentlands do feed the Clyde eventually. It is a thought which suddenly illuminates one more of the Pentlands' claims to fame: within that twenty miles swathe of small highlands are spawned waters which feed all three of south Scotland's great rivers – the Forth, the Tweed and the Clyde.

I like to throw a circle round that south-west corner from the Tarbrax road-end on the Lang Whang. The fact that the map identifies a right of way through the hills from here is no guarantee that a path is actually visible on the ground, and the line of aged posts which mark the line of the route are often as isolated as lighthouses, the path a frayed thread across the inevitable moorland and up the unpromising slouch of Henshaw Hill.

But as so often with the Pentlands, unpromising material bears surprising fruit, and on Henshaw's summit, a vast scope of the Pentlands unfurls. A small hollow by the summit is a good windbreak but it kills sound as well as wind and sightlines, and I emerged once to find a shepherd and his motorised three-wheeler bearing down on me with a startling turn of speed. He waved cheerfully enough and the vehicle coughed past, but it was a near miss by my reckoning, and my mood was not improved by the sudden stench of exhaust fumes on the still hill air.

I appreciate the worth of these machines to shepherds in terrain like this, but I loathe them for the brutal way they have of breaching the hill peace, of diminishing wildness, of distancing the shepherd from the hill ways. Many shepherds I have met have been good naturalists as well as sheep men, but how can you be a naturalist when you smash eyebright and cloudberry under wheels a foot wide? How do you cock an eye and an ear to the sight and sound of a displaying golden plover when your own presence is the loudest thing on the hill? How do you respond to the female's feigned broken wing when you have just driven over her nest? We have broken ties which once bound us to our animal origins, our closer ways with wildness. With vehicles like these, for all their convenience, we break a few more. Man has always shepherded flocks. Only in the last few years of all his history has he found it necessary to do so on wheels. Convenience should not be allowed to colour our every move in wild places. The wild places themselves still matter.

My south-west circle dips to the small spongy valley of the Garval Syke among the headwaters of the Medwin Water, then up the knee-jerking heathers of White Craig. The cairn stands above the curving trough of the Medwin which rings two-thirds of the hill like a moat. The effect is of a three-dimensional jigsaw puzzle in which the piece with White Craig on it has been shaken loose from its proper place leaving an awkward gap. The hill itself is a spur of Black Law, last resting place of Covenanter John Carphin, the summit ridge of a broad, level and airy walkway so typical of many of the Southern Pentland Hills. If you now tramp that crest, and if it is the Covenanter's Grave you seek, you will find yourself casting around uncertainly on the shoulder brow of Black Law. When you do find what you're looking for, you will be amazed how hard it was to find such a substantial stone.

I have never found the encounter with that stone unrewarding, never left the company of the Covenanter empty-handed, never ceased to marvel at Sanderson's act of profound charity, never failed to be moved by the power of the story. My circling drops to Sanderson's place which has somehow become a compulsory diversion after any visit to Black Law. It seems fitting to trek down to that Samaritan's threshold, because it is here that that remarkable story is completed, among the nettles and the ruinous fragments of Blackhill, the cottage Sanderson once called home. I make my own meagre tribute, I put a stone or two on the crumbling wall for The Artist, then I swing away to the west on an old green road which aims for the low profile of The Pike, but peters out before it gets there. The heather toughens and thickens and deepens and the hills gather briefly round, shutting out sightlines until I touch the summit of first The Pike, then Weather Law, and the sudden revelation of half of Scotland sounds a startled gasp in my throat. The Highland Hills are in snow, an unreal and disembodied frieze of sharp and intangible shapes, so small and so far away that they look as irrelevant to the Pentlands' scheme of things as the glimpsed shores of the Western Isles must have looked to the people of St. Kilda. Between those white summits and the Scottish Border, however, the land sprawls in wide moors, or plunges bluntly in shoals of whalebacks, and these the Pentlands wanderer can comprehend. These are the landscape kin of the Pentland Hills, the logical development of the hills as they evolve before him trekking south-west from Edinburgh, and which lead ultimately to this furthest south-west corner.

I have come at last to the loneliest acre of the hills, where the Crane Loch lies like a tiny flake of tinfoil in the low afternoon sun. I sit down in the broad swathe of boggy moor to the north of the loch and turn my glasses on its furtive

Roe deer are often seen among the woodlands at the edges of the Pentlands, and occasionally venture far out onto the heather moors to graze.

charms. There is no quieter shore in the Pentlands, and because a fluctuating population of wildfowl relishes that fact, I keep still and watch from a distance. Mallard and teal and a purposeful heron, a small knot of goldeneye, were all I could discern, but the trudge back across the moor is always good for a scattering of snipe or a dice with a hunting kestrel.

Once down by the Crane Loch, I watched two roe deer, trailing and grazing far out over the moor, a mile and more from their preferred woodland habitats down by Dunsyre or Boston Cottage. There is good grazing on the moors for roe, however, and The Artist and I came upon a pair away up the Medwin, watched their bouncing white rumps as they took to their heels in the most elegant of retreats.

The roe deer are the mute swans of the mammal kingdom – there is almost no action they perform which is not imbued with an instinctive and eloquent grace. To see them here, walking placidly uphill from the Crane Loch, unhurried and untroubled, the calf responding half-heartedly to the doe's barked summons, is a though-provoking moment. They *live* here. This is their world. They walk as readily to the Crane Loch as you or I might walk to the pub. Every day I am not here, their small rituals of living go on. The Crane Loch goes on filling and emptying itself of wildfowl. The Medwin goes on throbbing softly down to the West Water, to throw itself into the Clyde. The kestrels go swivelling up into the wind, and the voles go on threading the grasses until the last kestrel shadow falls on them, or a fox jaw darkens the end of their lives. I think about all that, and I think that it is a fleeting and perfunctory association I have with the Pentland Hills, because I come and go and stay away for days or weeks at a time, and all that time, there are small dramas of Pentland life which I am not there to see. I throw a last look at the silver loch, and as I leave, I leave a little more of me behind. Perhaps that is all any of us can ask.

CHAPTER 5

The Road Round the Hills

The road round the hills is also the road to the hills, and therein lies its double fascination. It is as we approach them, with high hopes and full of expectation, dreaming of the silent spaces of nature's wonderland which we are to explore, or returning full of peace and contentment, that unsuspectingly, the old travelling road will make its appeal to us. It is no ordinary road, this one round the hills. In some parts it is the old road of centuries modernised, in other parts the centuries-old road has grown green again, and its atmosphere disguised; it has all the charm and personality of old age grown beautiful and wise, to whose companionship wayfaring men now come as to a mother for counsel and consolation.

Will Grant, *The Call of the Pentlands.*

Will Grant devoted more than a third of his book to the road round the hills, a place of tramps and farriers and hawkers and horse-drawn this-and-thats, and only slowly, of the hesitant advance of motor traffic which now so rules and blurs the distinctions of the Pentlands' fringes.

Reith saw it coming, and bearing in mind that his book was published in 1910, the following is a remarkable prophecy: 'A few visitors spend the summer months in Carlops, but the accommodation is limited and of the simplest character. It is none the worse for that. If the village were more accessible and in closer touch with the busy world, it would be more patronised by the health-seeking townsman. For the last few years, coaches and motors have been running daily from Edinburgh during the summer, and these are rapidly making the place and its amenities known. Meanwhile, its scanty house-accommodation and its distance from railway and telegraph – over three miles – render it inconvenient to many who would otherwise seek summer quarters there. Some of us, however, for abominably selfish reasons, mildly hope that these inconveniences will not be removed yet awhile. A popularity entailing much new building and a crowd of summer residents would destroy the charm of this quaint old place in the eyes of those who love it best as it is.'

His fears were only slightly misdirected. Carlops has actually survived reasonably intact, except that the main road now carries an excruciating volume of traffic within a few feet of its 'quaint old' houses, and it is West Linton, two or three miles down the road, which the white settlers have colonised, and where they have more or less destroyed the charm.

And to both Reith and Grant, the fact that the road round the hills has now been overwhelmed at its northern end by the Edinburgh City Bypass would have been the stuff of incomprehensible nightmares. Times change. The tramps and hawkers have vanished with the farriers and horses. No more can a writer comment as Reith did that the tramp's 'greatest grievance against the existing cosmos is that the wayside inns will not open their bars to him before eight o' clock in the morning'. And you thought our licensing laws were liberal!

The road still has much to recommend it, though, not least a healthy repertoire of wayside inns, which, even if they won't serve you alcohol before eleven in the morning, are warmly hospitable for all that, and balm to many a Pentlands wanderer's hill thirst.

This sun-wise and subjective whistlestop of the road can be forgiven, I hope, for writing off everything between Bonaly and Hillend on the grounds that (the marooned charm of Swanston apart) neither the road nor the low hill ground have anything to recommend them. But south of Hillend, the road assumes tolerable proportions and begins to hug the hills in a more endearing fashion, begins to hint at roadside fascinations.

The old church and burial ground of Glencorse, mulled

Glencorse Church ... pride of place in the roll call of Pentlands kirks and kirkyards.

over by Stevenson until the day he died on the other side of the world, is the first of these. There are as many intriguing kirks and kirkyards about the hills as there are inns, and Stevenson has seen to it that Glencorse has pride of place in their roll call.

The place is ruinous now, and much too troubled by the clamour of traffic and creeping development to evoke as much of a presence as Stevenson could divine, and its finest hours are best left to him, the hour, for instance, when he sat listening to one Mr Torrence preaching, one Sunday in 1875; '... his voice leapt like an ill-played clarionet from key to key – over eighty and a relic of times forgotten, with his black thread gloves and mild old foolish face.'

And in a letter home from Samoa, he wrote: 'Do you know that the dearest burn to me in the world is that which drums and pours in cunning whimples in that glen of yours behind Glencorse Old Kirk? Oh that I were a lad I once was,

Flotterstone – a good inn, a fine bridge and a base and information centre for the Pentland Hills Regional Park. Reproduced by courtesy of the Edinburgh Photographic Library.

sitting under old Torrence, that old shepherd of let-well-alone, and watching with awe the waving of the old black gloves over the Bible – the preacher's white finger-ends meanwhile aspiring through! Do you know where the road crosses the burn under Glencorse Church? Go there and say a prayer for me. See it is a sunny day; would like it to be a Sunday; but that's not possible in the premises; and stand on the right bank, and shut your eyes; and – if I don't appear to you!'

Flotterstone is one of those good Pentlands inns, hard by the Glencorse Burn and one of those staunch old bridges which the builders of the road round the hills had to sling over temperamental hill burns every few miles. The regional park has laid on an information centre here, complete with weather forecast, ranger base, woodland trail, picnic tables, and all the other bric-a-brac of the 'civilised' countryside which encourages the notion that since the car was invented most people who drive to the countryside don't stray more than quarter of a mile from the car park. So there's a car park too. It should be said that the facilities are good and well planned and thoughtful, and if there have to be such facilities, they are rarely done better than this. My problem is that I have never yet heard a convincing argument which justifies them.

Flotterstone's best-kept secret, however, was another countryside facility of a sort, I suppose, a forty-feet wide stone circle which once stood on what Grant describes a bit vaguely as 'the west side of Flotterstone brae'. Whether he means the road, or the hill behind Flotterstone, or possibly both, is unclear, and the name has long since disappeared from maps if it was ever on one. He rages briefly at the dismantling of the circle to build a dyke (a common enough fate of prehistoric works from Shetland to Land's End), but beyond that, quotes no source or reference and hurries on breathlessly. I want to stop him there, pin him to the wall and question him vigorously, but he is gone and I have found no other straw to clutch at, no other reference to his circle.

But such a circle, say on a knoll above the inn, would be no more than a mile from Castlelaw, half a mile from the fort above Lawhead Farm, a mile from the cup and ring marks at Glencorse Kirkyard, a mile from the cairn on Carnethy. A centrepiece? If so, of what purpose, and who built it? You scratch the surface of these things at your peril, for all that spills out is a procession of questions. Even such majestic survivals as the Ring of Brodgar in Orkney have baffled the best of historians, so what hope for a circle which has become the straight line of a dyke up a flank of the Pentlands?

Here, on this road around the hills, we may be nearer to an explanation of sorts than we imagine. The Lothian and Borders volume of the exemplary HMSO series of books

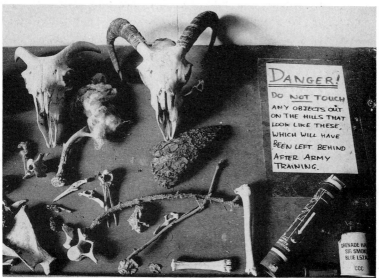

Pointed souvenirs of the hills – of one kind or another – are displayed at the Flotterstone Visitor Centre.

The start of the Kirk Road path near Silverburn. The path crosses the hills between Carnethy and Scald Law, and was used by hill folk on the way to church in Penicuik.

Exploring Scotland's Heritage suggests that the road has been going round the hills for rather longer than we might think. Referring to a cluster of cairns around Dolphinton, its author John R. Baldwin writes: 'This chain of large, round prehistoric cairns in the Dolphinton-West Linton area (there are other more elevated examples on such Pentland summits as East Cairn Hill, West Cairn Hill, and Carnethy Hill), seems to mark an important prehistoric route linking the upper Clyde Valley with the Forth estuary. It would have left the Clyde at its junction with the Medwin Water, skirted the south-west of the Pentlands and then followed their south-east flanks before cutting across the River North Esk – where similar cairns existed near Roslin and Rosewell.'

So, for whatever reason, the cairn builders didn't fancy the Cauldstane Slap either, though it would have greatly shortened their route. Too many bears, perhaps! One or two of the surviving cairns are mightily impressive, but having stood in something approaching sacred awe among standing stones at Brodgar, how I wish Flotterstone's stone ring had survived. Cairns don't own half the mysteries of a stone ring.

The modern road holds hard to the skirts of Carnethy and Scald Law, blurs through Silverburn, after which it parallels a Roman road which clings in turn to a higher fold of the skirts. This is where the old road has 'grown green again', as Grant put it, and from here to Dolphinton there are snatches and stretches and long swacks of much older thoroughfares above today's road. None of them is dull, they all throw sightlines to and from the hills, and in their more charismatic stretches you can feel as if you have somehow parted from the ways of modern man and stumbled on the remnants of an older order of things.

It is, at its best, a fleeting illusion, because sooner or later you will have to step aside for a tractor, or a combine, or a Land-Rover, but if you are lucky, as I once was on a misted April morning, you'll walk an entranced mile in which the hill tops – but only the hill tops – were slowly unwrapped by

The sign above the door of Habbie's Howe inn at Nine Mile Burn commemorates the poet Allan Ramsay and his best-known work, 'The Gentle Shepherd'. The sign reads: 'Gan farrer down the Burn tae Habbies Howe, Whaur a' the sweets o Summer grow, and when yer tired o prattlin side the rill, Return to Nine Mile Burn and tak a gill'.

The Gentle Shepherd inspired many place names around the village of Carlops, and drouthy visitors and villagers repair to the Allan Ramsay inn.

the sun's burgling fingers, and the only traffic I encountered was two horsemen who emerged from the mist, spoke a monosyllabic greeting and greyly dematerialised into the mist over my shoulder.

I stopped and listened as the sound of the hooves echoed down the road I had just walked, and in that moment's fey stillness, I gathered its sounds about me: a far farm dog barked three times, a cock pheasant pooh-poohed the presence of a rival, a tiny burn ran over a six-inch fall, trees dripped. Every sound magnified only the silence in which it was set, and I dwelt briefly in another time.

It is a gift of the Pentland Hills, this dislocation of the senses, which never fails to catch me unawares, and you need the milestone names of Eight Mile Burn and Nine Mile Burn to remind you how near you are to that other world of Edinburgh. You are not just as near as that, however, because when these names were conferred we all used Scots miles, which were worth a bit more than English ones. Well, they would be, wouldn't they? If you would like

A tree nursery at Glencorse growing species native to Pentlands area.
The decline of the hills' woodland is a matter for real concern.

to know how much more, Nine Mile Burn is eleven-and-three-quarter English miles from Edinburgh, so you can work it out for yourself. My maths gets me as far as one-and-a-bit.

The name 'Habbie's Howe' on the inn at Nine Mile Burn signposts not just the most hospitable of all Pentlands howffs but also your entry into the country of *The Gentle Shepherd,* a minor literary phenomenon of the eighteenth century. *The Gentle Shepherd* was a 'pastoral comedy' written by the Edinburgh poet Allan Ramsay. The play, written in 1725, with a ballad-opera version four years later, stamped its linguistic authority on the writing of Scots as a language for many generations, but its effect on the countryside around Carlops (where the play is set) has been as enduring as it is astounding. In Carlops itself you drink in the Allan Ramsay. Habbie's Howe is a waterfall on the North Esk at Newhall to the north-east of the village, but it was Ramsay who christened it. If it had a name before 1725, it has long since been forgotten. All around Carlops are farm and landscape names like Roger's Rig, Scroggy Brae, Paties Mill, Peggy's Lea and Habbie's Howe itself (though Ramsay wrote it Habby's How), all of them named after characters or places in *The Gentle Shepherd,* all of them given the seal of permanent approval by the Ordnance Survey.

The play itself is lightweight, and its language – a hybrid of workaday Scots, affected Scots, and aristocratic English – makes it difficult for today's ears, but if you take the rhythmic sweep of it and follow the sense of the dialogue rather than dissecting it line by line with a Scots dictionary in your hand, you'll find a vigorous period piece and a richness of language which left its mark on both Burns and the street-wise poetry of Robert Fergusson. A sample, with Peggy and Jenny at

'A flowrie howm between twa verdent braes,
Where lasses use to wash and spread their claiths…'

West Linton Kirk. Reproduced by courtesy of Scotland in Focus, Galashiels.

Jenny – Come, Meg, let's fa' to work upon this green,
    The shining day will bleech our linen clean;
    The water's clear, the lift unclouded blew,
    Will make them lilly wet with dew.

Peggy – Go farer up the burn to Habby's How,
    Where a' the sweets of spring and summer grow;
    Between twa birks, out o'er a little lin
    The water fa's, and makes a singand din;
    A pool breast-deep beneath, as clear as glass
    Kisses with easy whirles the bordring grass;
    We'll end our washing while the morning's cool,
    And when the day grows het, we'll to the pool,
    There wash our sells – 'tis healthfu' now in May,
    And sweetly cauler on sae warm a day.'

116

West Linton, where an old kirkyard has a rich repertoire of carved stones: 'the old sculptors cocked a gleeful snook at death with skulls and crossbones and hourglasses and gruesome effigies ....'

Waterfall, Glencorse Burn.

The sign over the door of the Habbie's Howe inn gives a neat parodied twist to Peggy's first four lines.

Inevitably, when Edinburgh began to discover Carlops, about the time Reith was sounding his dire warnings, it was to Habbie's Howe that the crowds flocked, with, according to Reith, unsavoury consequence for the quality of the water. How he put it was this: 'It is much patronised by picnickers in the summer-time, and on their account no modern Peggy or Jenny dare now bathe in that limpid pool "when the day grows het".'

Carlops still manages to keep a calm souch, as Ramsay might have said. It remains a place inextricably entwined with the Pentlands, a hillside village surrounded by soft, secretive places, brown trout stream pools where you can still bathe discreetly, welcoming woodlands, and all of it well washed by the hill winds.

The main road makes for West Linton, the old road burrows deep into the hill flank, and the fine wee pass of Windy Gowl burrows deeper still under Mount Maw, and joins a short cut to the Cauldstane Slap. West Linton feels curiously detached from the hills, its narrow and grey streets exert an introverted influence, and the hills themselves are shuttered by woods. It was once the hub of a far-reaching web of drove roads, and although both coach road and railway gave it an unaccountably wide berth, that did not stop the inhabitants of yore from describing their village as 'the Sub-Metropolitan of Tweeddale' ('whatever that may mean,' Reith remarked dryly). It was certainly a cattle and sheep market of no meagre significance until the mid-nineteenth century when it was usurped by Lanark. Its social standing has been devalued these days to a small commuter outpost for Edinburgh, and the new housing developments alongside the golf course road suggest nothing so much as a transplanted Edinburgh suburb.

Still, the old village has good pubs, a connoisseur's tearoom, and one of those intriguing kirkyards where the old tombstone sculptors cocked a gleeful snook at death

A stretch of the West Linton Road near Silverburn. The name remains a mystery; there's no record of silver mining nearby, just a legend about a crock of gold.

Spittal, a hill farm on the slopes above Nine Mile Burn.

with skulls and crossbones and hourglasses and gruesome effigies, all carved with telling skill. Inside, the church is distinguished by particularly handsome wood carving and a startlingly modern stained-glass window.

The road round the hills becomes briefly a threefold road south of West Linton, where the Old Biggar Road and the Roman road part company, but all three roads more or less coincide again near Dolphinton. Transport seems to have made something of a habit of homing in on Dolphinton for no good reason. Apart from the example of the cairn builders, there is surely no less likely location for *two* railway stations. There are none now, of course, but as Reith records (not without his customary jibe at all things preposterous), 'about three miles from West Linton, the two railway termini of Dolphinton are reached. This sounds imposing, but as the termini are two forlorn little shanties on opposite sides of the high-road, the imposingness looks a bit of an imposition. The one is the terminus of a little branch of the North British Railway's line into Peebles. (The frivolous may call it a twig.) The other is a Caledonian branch from Carstairs. Why a hamlet of half a dozen houses should have two rival stations puzzles the casual visitor, but the existing situation is the result of Parliamentary compromise between the rival companies, both of which, for reasons which are not obvious to the uninititiated, were extremely anxious to get to Dolphinton. Now that they have got there, they do not seem to have made much of it. The real reason for this wasteful rivalry seems to have been that the North British were very anxious to get into Lanarkshire and the Caledonian were equally anxious to keep them out. At present, in Dolphinton, they are like the pickets of opposing armies, who fraternise and exchange flasks till the battle begins.'

Although two termini at Dolphinton does sound like at least one too many, it is sad that several generations have now grown up quite oblivious to the rumbling, reeking charms of small rural trains. The Pentlands used to be

Mendick Hill dominates the south-east corner of the Pentlands, a familiar landmark to travellers on the Old Biggar Road.

ringed by railways, and the thoughtless severing of their lifelines has often been the first step in the demise of many small communities, and in many a Scottish landscape at that. Rural buses and Postbuses have made something of a comeback in the last few years, but it is too little too late for many a hamlet, and the railways, like the oldest roads round the hills, have grown green again.

The road burrows deep into the hills again, forsaking the modern main road to Carnwath in favour of a secretively wooded way to Dunsyre. The high point of the road, at about 900ft, unwraps the southern frontier of the Pentlands from the handsome Mendick Hill to Horse Law, and the dark mass of Craigengar and Byrehope Mount. The centrepiece of this first and last gesture of the Pentland Hills, however, is the green thrust of Dunsyre Hill. It is a modest 1313 feet, but its lapel badge scree and its fort-sculpted summit impart a landscape status which belies its height. It is a lynchpin place, Dunsyre Hill, and whether you start or end your Pentlands here, it is the perfect summit.

Dunsyre may or may not mean the hill fort of the seer, but

Dunsyre Hill, the southmost summit of the Pentlands: 'whether you start or end your Pentlands here, it is the perfect summit'. The name may well mean 'the hill fort of the seer'.

one who believes it 'because I want to' is The Artist. In a previous incarnation of mine, when I commissioned him to scribble this-and-thats for the Edinburgh *Evening News*, he wrote a telling little series on the Pentlands, telling because it unearthed as much as anything his own infectious and captivatingly expressed love and pride and prejudices amid these hills. So he interviewed the then minister of Dunsyre, Dolphinton and Elsrickle, James Ballantyne, '... larger than life and hugely eccentric for his age ... a direct descendant of the Reverend Patrick Anderson, the Covenanting preacher'.

The Artist wrote of him thus: 'A man of many projects, he pioneered the use of the cine camera in archaeological digs; introduced the inkle loom to Africa and encouraged the bairns of the Sunday school to use it in the weaving of their very own tartan.

'The black stripe represents the Black Mount – a favourite place of conventicles. The purple is the heather. Blue, the river and white for the snow. Red for the red roads of

Dunsyre Kirk, an elegantly simple church with a matchless setting. It is here that the original Covenanter's Grave, carved by Sanderson, is now kept.

The sculptor's art is well displayed among the quiry headstones in Dunsyre's kirkyard.

Dunsyre, and gold for the cornfields.'

'It was his passion for archaeology which drove him to excavate his church floor some years back. "Yes, it was a wee bit naughty of me, I suppose, but I wheeched the floor out and found a sepulchral grave. And you know, when we opened it, we found the skeleton of a bandy-legged dwarf. He must have been a very important man, because the other bodies had been placed around him fan-wise. Dwarfs were often revered, you know, in religion. They had them in Bhuddhist monasteries in the Himalayas. They represented the petty annoyances and grievances of life ... people would kick these poor souls up the behind because of this."

' "Who do you think this VIP dwarf was, then? Your actual Seer of Dunsyre?" I asked facetiously.

' "No ... no. Well, it could ... might well have been. But don't write that down. It's just a daft notion of mine." God bless your daft notions, James Ballantyne.'

So The Artist and his seer theory had a powerful ally and who am I to dispute the findings of such a meeting of minds? The sadness about Dunsyre today is that its sublime

One of the headstones in Dunsyre kirkyard, nicknamed 'The Goalie' by the author and his friend George Garson. This is George Garson' drawing of a stone with a profound personal significance.

little church is what is euphemistically known in church circles as redundant. The delight is that the church is still open to discreet visitors, still lovingly maintained, and a fit resting place for Sanderson's original stone which marked the Covenanter's Grave on Black Law. It is an uncut boulder into which Sanderson ingeniously carved his untutored tribute to the Covenanter in a coded arrangement of letters.

I'm not much of a haunter of old kirks and kirkyards and I'm more likely to find my definition of such Gods as I hold

The homely and hospitable thatch of another fine wee inn on the road round the hills, the Wee Bush Inn at Carnwath, where Burns is reputed to have paused and scratched one of his many window verses.

to up-by on the unsanctified tops of the Pentlands. But once in a while I've stumbled on a set of conducive circumstances which conferred a certain sacred credibility on a building with aspirations to be a House of God. At Dunsyre, the simplicity of the church and its calm landscape setting, the quirky headstones on their wooded knoll, the sough of the hill winds, all conspire to invoke a rare sense of peace. I can readily concede that a spiritual presence is a fundamental component of that peace.

The Artist has marked one of the headstones for a small ritual when the Great Muralist is the Sky finally calls him for the Private View to end all private views, and we're to cast his ashes into the charge of a character long since dubbed The Goalie by we Dunsyre addicts. The Goalie is carved on his own headstone, facing the best shots of the west wind. He stands arms wide, hands low, legs bent in a purposeful, intent crouch in his baggy shorts. The initials SM are about his head (or hers, perish the thought!) and 1782 at his feet.

The more I step softly about that tranquil place, the more I invest him with the authority of some kind of guardian spirit of his unlikely goalmouth. Sometimes I wish I knew who he was, and what he was. Sometimes, though, I am just as pleased that I don't and I celebrate his enigma. Once I thought he might be the wee dwarf from under the floorboards, but don't write that down, it's just a daft notion of mine....

I never forgot that it was The Artist who introduced us, and that this is his soul country rather than mine, but the introduction was effected with such infectious generosity that an awful lot has rubbed off.

The true road round the hills westers only another mile, then cuts north-west to Boston Cottage on the Lang Whang. On the way it passes Stonypath where artist and poet Ian Hamilton Finlay tends a garden of astounding richness under the disapproving bulk of Bleak Law. The silk purse from a sow's ear theory is in shreds at Stonypath.

Another old drove road slips between Horse Law and Left Law (which is inevitably on the right) and makes for the Lang Whang. Meanwhile, the driving road has ducked down to Carnwath where the Edinburgh Road and the Lanark Road go their separate ways. Carnwath is the kind of small town for which the Scots tongue might have specifically invented the word 'couthy'. You find such places all over rural Scotland, small, self-contained places, hospitable communities which grew up in simpler eras. Reith could write of his turn-of-the-century era, for example, that: 'Within memory of a few still living, the town-drummer used to go around the streets at 5 a.m. waking the inhabitants to get their cattle out. The town-herd followed him and drove the cattle to the common pasture.'

Given that a few still living might just remember Reith himself, what an astounding leap of living history that is! Today's Carnwath boasts one of the finest wee inns anywhere in the Wee Bush Inn. It's one of the many howffs where Burns is reputed to have scratched a verse on the window,

West Linton, once the hub of a web of far-reaching drove roads. Lady Gifford, wife of one of West Linton's most famous lairds, clings to the clock tower above her "well".

The Bavelaw marshes at Thriepmuir Reservoir are often an autumn and winter haunt of migrating whooper swans. Here a small gathering takes advantage of midwinter sunshine.

but who cares? What matters is a welcoming ambience, a stone floor, a fire, a thatched roof and the kind of food and drink which sustains a traveller and lures him back. I fancy it was to this howff that Will Grant repaired back in the days when you could still get up to escapades like this:

'This was my experience one autumn day. I missed the track soon after crossing the Medwin, and found the heather track knee-deep for miles. It would be better, one thought, to strike the Lang Whang where the going would be better, now that it was past sunset and dusk would soon be gathering, but no sign of a road could be discerned. I rested and listened; there was a silence everywhere on this evening of an Indian summer day. Then a faint sound of a farm cart on rough road, but that cart seemed a long way off. I continued the heather step, determined to find the road if possible. In a short time I came upon the Lang Whang which I welcomed as a friend. The tall heather had hidden it completely from view. Soon I met two country folks and on inquiring how far it was to Carnwath was told it was about five miles. Five miles

Ancient Malleny House and its Garden are now owned by the National Trust for Scotland. The Garden is one of Balrno's chief attractions and, besides its clipped yews, has one of the best collections of shrub roses in the east of Scotland. Courtesy National Trust for Scotland.

more after so many did not matter much and I felt relieved. After tramping about two more miles I again made inquiry of two fishers on a stream near by. But fishers have no idea of distance, they were intent on getting trout before darkness came down, and again I was informed it was about five miles. Well, well, I thought, I am at least holding my own. Then the September moon rose, and cheerily I swung down into Carnwath. Two things were needful, food and a railway time-table. While greedily satisfying a ravenous appetite in the inn, I inquired if there was a train that night to Edinburgh. Yes, there was a train. "And when does it start?" "In ten minutes." " And how far is it to the station?" "About a mile." "But I can't walk a mile in ten minutes," I expostulated.

' "Oh," replied the innkeeper, "but there's a short-cut through the wood." "Is it a dark wood?" "Aye, it's gey dark, gey dark, but there's a mune the nicht."

Old wooden weekend shacks gather in little shanty towns around some of the Pentlands fringes. This one is near Carlops.

'I left the inn hurriedly, caught hold of a boy at the door, and pressed him into service to show me the road through the wood. We arrived at the station where faint lights glimmered from the oily lamps but no sound was heard. "Are you sure there is another train, my lad?" I asked eagerly. "Oh aye," he replied, "but it's sometimes late an' it doesna maitter much, there's naebody traivillin'".

'So I waited in the silent frost night, and the train came, a special: at least it stopped specially, or only for me. I was glad, for it had been a long day, but a glorious one, and I did it all alone, and that's why I remember every step of it, although it happened a quarter of a century ago....'

Attitudes towards the Lang Whang depend on how you feel about long horizon-topping straights, fistfuls of wet winds which can punch a car sideways, miles-wide moors and a low-profile approach to the hills. I have always loved hills which you can approach from afar, watching them grow, feeling their influence strengthen its grip. The Pentlands from the Lang Whang are like that. The road is distinguished enough to merit its own definition in *The Concise Scots Dictionary*. The entry under 'whang' reads: 'a long stretch of rather narrow road, *specif* the Lang Whang the old Edinburgh to Lanark road, *esp* between Balerno and Carnwath.'

Today, the road tramps towards Balerno past the hidden fragments of one of the most frightening schemes never to see the light of day, the proposed road through the Cauldstane Slap. Many a crackpot has talked about such a thing for two hundred years and more, but the closest it came to reality was the beginning of a viaduct near the farms of Causewayend in the 1830s, and the rich and influential on both sides of the hills got the bit between their teeth. The Earl of Morton would have none of it, not on his land, he thundered, and the scheme was mercifully scuppered. It would be nice to think we have all learned enough since then to ensure that it will never happen now. Wouldn't it be nice to think that?

You are almost back in Edinburgh's embrace and beginning to think, perhaps, that the Pentlands have finished with you, when you slip off the main road of an August evening of heady, musky stillness, and catch up with a snatch of the Old Lanark Road hard under the hills. There in a last and memorable gesture of the Pentland Hills, you encounter the furthest fringe of the Edinburgh Festival Fringe, the Bonnie Blooming Heather Show.

Edinburgh's Festival heart pulsates nine miles and a throbbing city world away from the Red Moss, a purpling late-August splash colour-washing the feet of the Pentlands by Balerno, a glowing heathery festival in its own right. The road round the hills here is at its oldest, a dye-straight two-mile scrap of that Old Lanark Road that was, before Balerno mushroomed itself into an Edinburgh afterthought, and we invented the A70. Where the old road passes Red Moss, its travellers rub shoulders with an exhibition of living, growing, breathing, dying, unfettered by any frame, the subtle art of the raised bog.

Red Moss is a domed bog, thatched thick and deep with heather, laced with mosses, flowers and grasses, cushioned by a layer of water and 18 feet of peat, its surface fragile as an inch of ice. Nature has carefully arranged that the heathery blaze is at its height during the Edinburgh Festival. One of the stars of the show is sundew, an ingenious bog-loving gem which fools flies and midges for a living and fooled bygone generations of naturalists into calling it sundew. The trick is in the pinky-green cluster of hairy leaves round the base of the stem. Every hair on every leaf holds a tiny shining droplet. 'Water,' concludes the midge knowing water to be the habitat in with midge eggs are laid.

'Wrong,' counters the sundew, and holds the bewildered midge in its sticky clasp, extracts such minute delicacies as it requires and discards the carcase, all of which is no more than the average midge deserves. They say one sundew accounts for 2000 insects in a summer, but from the midge hordes which still cluster over Red Moss on a still summer

Several stretches of the old road south still hug the lower slopes of the hills – this one is between Nine Mile Burn and Carlops.

evening, the world is desperately short of sundew. But back to the droplets.

'Dew,' concluded the naturalist of yesteryear, 'and the plant retains it even in strong sunlight ... so, sundew!' And so the lie was given birth. 'It has magic powers,' concluded the alchemist, 'the dew burns off warts.' 'The dew,' concluded the herbalist, 'will excite lust in cattle.' 'Wrong, wrong, wrong' sighed the sundew, and went on slaying insects by the thousand.

There are other small deaths. The Scottish Wildlife Trust, which manages Red Moss as a nature reserve, held an open day there once and featured the complete skeleton of a woodmouse, pieced together from a short-eared owl pellet. It may not be everyone's idea of Festival art, but I can think of many a painting and sculpture with less to recommend them. And when the Festival rolls out of town dragging its seasonal migration of culture vultures at heel, the Red Moss dons the garb of a new season and puts on a new show. It has gone on for 5000 years, and all without the assistance of the Scottish Arts Council.

Balerno is the end of the road round the hills, and the only one of that long-lost string of villages which once began at Colinton to feel even remotely part of the Pentland landscape. Colinton, Currie and Juniper Green have grown anonymous as Corstorphine, their village-ness engulfed, their Pentland-ness overwhelmed by their Edinburgh-ness. At Balerno, though, the hills are still – just – a tangible presence, and the impression is still of a community which tries to look south to the hills, rather than north-east to the city.

Reith had it in for Balerno, and wrote thus: 'Balerno village offers little interest to the passer-by. It stands chiefly on two sides of a steep street, and is mainly remarkable for not having anything you may happen to want. Having forgotten to take a handkerchief with me one morning, I visited all the shops in search of that useful article, but found it not. One may draw several inferences from that fact, most

There is much fragmentary evidence of old rural industry around the Pentlands, like these ruined limekilns on the Deep Syke burn near Carlops.

of them probably wrong.' We can infer for sure, though, that Mr. Reith was not one to wipe his nose on the sleeves of his jacket. On that most of Edinburgh notes, the road is done.

CHAPTER 6

The Future of the Hills

The Pentland Hills will always be blessed and cursed by the proximity of Edinburgh, but provided the city extends its territorial ambitions no further than the new bypass, the blessings should always outnumber the curses.

The curses are the obvious ones.

Firstly, there will always be a problem in the northern Pentlands of too many people for the good of the hills.

Secondly, the country parks at Hillend and Bonaly have introduced an urban playground mentality into the hills which is dangerous because it trivialises the hills and because it will almost certainly spread: there is nothing new about proposals to join the two country parks together. The one certain consequence of providing facilities on the ground in the countryside is a campaign for bigger and better facilities. On hill ground like the Pentlands, the two have never mixed well and they never will.

Thirdly, there is the Pentland Hills Regional Park. I will give the park short shrift here, because I have already registered disapproval enough.

I once asked a representative of the park – at a conference called The Wild Lothians – why there should be a park at all. I was told that the question was mischievous and politically motivated, and on every subsequent occasion I have sought an answer to the question, I have heard nothing which did not either similarly evade it, or which did not answer it in such a welter of bureaucratspeak as to be utterly unintelligible. The park is an imposed regime, neither asked for nor elected, its authority self-appointed, its concept is alien to the Scottish countryside, it is expensive and remote, it has offered no shred of landscape protection, its effect has been to dilute the wildness of the Pentlands within its control, and any serious contemplation of the future of the Pentlands must begin by scrapping it. Shrift doesn't come much shorter than that.

So much for the curses of Edinburgh's proximity. The blessings are these:

Firstly, it was Edinburgh's coterie of literary figures which won the hills their fame and gave them a pedigree no other small range of low hills enjoys. In doing so, they ensured that the Pentlands would also be revered by future generations of their readers. No other Scottish city has performed that service for its landscape setting.

Secondly, the growth of Edinburgh to its present size has provided a much larger reservoir of goodwill towards the Pentlands. Edinburgh is by-and-large a city which is conscious of its own environment, and any city which is conscious of its own environment, and any city which cherishes a mountain at its heart can only look with favour on the hills beyond its doorstep. As I have suggested in Chapter 2, the Edinburgh people have a warm regard for the Pentlands simply because of that benevolent presence crouching along the city's southern skyline. In many people, it is an unthinking warmth, for they will live all their lives in Edinburgh and never set a foot in the Pentlands, yet because the hill's shape is part of the psyche of being an Edinburgher, he will always spring to their defence. Many others, though, know and love the Pentlands all their lives, cross and re-cross them, discover and re-discover them. Their loyalty is especially fierce.

Thirdly, that loyalty translates to a demonstrable concern for the principles of wise conservation. Edinburgh has the biggest concentration in Scotland of conservation enthusiasts and members of conservation organisations. When I worked as a features writer for the *Edinburgh Evening News*, and wondered how I might turn my campaigning instincts into constructive resistance to the then proposed regional park, I was first overwhelmed, then encouraged and sustained, by the support of readers. Four years of writing a

wildlife column there had already alerted me to the recep-
tive nature of the audience, but the threat to the Pentlands
touched a raw nerve end, and Edinburgh howled its opposition. Alas, the park manufacturers preferred to listen to
themselves rather than the people of Edinburgh, or for that
matter the people who lived around and in the hills
themselves.

Friends of the Pentlands in both Edinburgh and the
communities around the hills have a healthy disregard for
the park and tend to see it as nothing more than a tempo-
rary intrusion, a trespasser in their landscape to be evicted
in time if it proves too troublesome. More likely, it will self-
destruct once the Scottish countryside 'establishment' re-
organises itself and deflects its enthusiasm into another fad,
or the money runs out, or both. That portion of the
Pentlands outwith the park is conspicuously wilder, quieter,
healthier, more natural.

But if not a park, what? What preoccupies many people
who go on the hills today, both in the Pentlands and
beyond, is how best to safeguard the future of the hills,
honouring their wildness, sustaining the Scottish traditions
of freedom to roam and closeness to the land, and beginning to repay the debt we owe hills like the Pentlands. Is
there any necessity for change at all to achieve that, beyond
a return to the pre-park status quo? Is every man for himself
and every landowner for himself not good enough?

I think not. The voice of the professional countryside
establishment bureaucrat is articulate, persuasive, well fi-
nanced (often by public money), well publicised and well
trained. It is also usually strident and wrong. Certainly it is
deaf to the myriad voices of hill people and utterly insensi-
tive to the needs of the landscape itself.

But I think there is need for an organisation which
springs from the Pentlands people, those who live within
the sight and sound and smell and 'force field' of the hills.
It should be dedicated to the cause of the wellbeing of the
hills themselves, and for their own sake. It is a suggestion I

advance with some trepidation because there are already far too many conservation groups in existence, because I am the least committed of committee-minded people, because I know from sorrowful experience the trials of starting a new organisation from scratch with the highest of ideals and seeing the ideals diluted by people who found them too high to live up to and lowered them to a common denominator with which they felt comfortable. A conservation group which feels comfortable with itself is not doing its job. It is not easy to champion a piece of wild countryside and be relentless in its defence.

Nevertheless, and knowing how wrong it can all go, I believe that the Pentlands need all the friends they can get. Their best hope is that those Pentlands people who love them best are given a voice, and that that voice can become a significant pressure group to be considered thoughtfully by those who own and manage the Pentland Hills, and those politicians whose responsibilities impinge on the Pentland Hills.

Such a group (call it The Friends of the Pentlands for argument's sake) could carry much more weight than something like the park because it would articulate the collective voice of the people who know and love and cherish the hills for their own sake, and not because they are paid to give lip service to part of them. It would also articulate the voice of the electorate, which is always a more worrying voice in the ear of local and national politicians than a quango.

That is the theory. The practice would depend on the right kind of people shaping and effecting policies and priorities. If the priority is to be the wellbeing of the hills, then the leaders of any Friends of the Pentlands should be those whose love for and knowledge of the hills is deepest-seated, those who were born and brought up with the hills and born into their particularly Scottish traditions. Un-Scottish voices and attitudes often win more enemies than friends in Scottish conservation circles, and it is important that any leadership group reflects not just the people who live around the Pentlands, but laso the sense of place which is unique to the Pentlands. There are many 'professional committee. people' among conservation groups in Scotland, and in my experience of them, they should be avoided at all costs. The first criterion should be a long track record of devotion to the Pentland Hills, a profound respect for their wildness, traditions and Scottishness.

As to the policies and priorities of the Friends of the Pentlands, they could do worse than consider the creed in operation at Ferniehaugh: look after the elements – the skyline, the heather, the water, the trees, the dykes, for if all these are in good heart, the Pentlands will be in good heart. To that list, the Friends might add the cross-Pentlands footpaths because, uniquely among Scottish Hills, they are a fundamental part of the Pentlands and of the essential experience of being among these hills.

If championing the Pentlands' elements is to be the first commandment of any new organisation, it follows that it should also resist threats to the wellbeing of the elements, a diverse list which will change from time to time but which should include the park, the presence of the Army, bad landowning practice, bulldozed roads like the monster of Black Hill, destructive events like the Pentlands Skyline Race (bewilderingly sponsored in 1990 by the Edinburgh *Evening News* which once campaigned against the regional park), mountain bikes, formal organised recreation, and any other irritants or intrusions which despoil the wildness of the hills.

There is endless scope in the service of the Pentland Hills for such an organisation. It can educate. It can lobby. It can propose its own ideas for wiser management, and may even eventually be able to implement them. It can promote the needs of wildlife and help to enhance and diversify wildlife habitats. Because of the compact nature of the Pentlands it could learn quickly of new threats such as housing and leisure developments, and if necessary campaign against them.

It is a job, almost certainly unpaid, for people with commitment, tact, tenacity, an ability to impress landowners and local authorities and many other shades of opinion and vested interest. It is also a job which will mean taking an uncompromising stand against those whose actions are against the best interests of the hills.

Stevenson said it a hundred years ago: 'It seems as if it must come to an open fight at last to preserve a corner of green country unbedevilled.'

Where the need for that fight arises now – and it will arise more and more – the voice of the unrepresented hill man and the voice of the Pentland Hills should be heard. The way for it to be heard is to give it a mouthpiece.

It bears repeating that the first and last and most important qualities for such a fight are a profound and lifelong love of the hills themselves, a passion for a corner of green country unbedevilled, an addiction to the Pentland Wine.

Further Reading

Baldwin, John R. *Exploring Scotland's Heritage,* Lothian
and the Borders volume (HMSO 1985)

Cochrane, Robert *Pentland Walks with their Literary and
Historical Associations* (Andrew Elliot 1930)

Grant, Will *The Call of the Pentlands* (Robert Grant 1927)
Pentland Days and Country Ways (Nelson 1934)

Munro, Ian *The Birds of the Pentland Hills* (Scottish
Academic Press 1988)

Ramsay, Allan and Fergusson, Robert *Poems by Allan
Ramsay and Robert Fergusson* (Scottish Academic Press
1985)

Reith, George M. The Breezy Pentlands (Foulis 1910)

Stevenson, R.L. *Picturesque Old Edinburgh* (Albyn Press
1983)

Index